Lovers Take up Less Space

An alphabet guide to the Tube

Rosemary J. Kind

Copyright © 2011 Rosemary J. Kind

All rights reserved. Any unauthorised broadcasting, public performance, copying or recording will constitute an infringement of copyright. No part of this book may be reproduced or transmitted in any form or by any means, electronically or mechanical, including photocopying, fax, data transmittal, internet site, recording or any information storage or retrieval system without the express written permission of the publisher except for the use of brief quotations in a book review.

Printed in the United Kingdom

First Printing, 2011 Alfie Dog Limited

The author can be contacted at: authors@alfiedog.com

Cover image: Sessha Batto

ISBN 978-1-909894-34-1

Published by
Alfie Dog Limited
Rose Bank, Norton Lindsey,
Warwickshire, CV35 8JQ
Tel: 07712 647754

DEDICATION

To *Transport for London*, for the amazing feat that is the London Underground.

But also to you, the tightly packed and slightly frayed passengers, without your sweat, stares, jostling, and peculiar habits, this book would never have come into being.

Thank you,

RJK

CONTENTS

Acknowledgments	i
Introduction	1
Lovers Take Up Less Space	5
Alphabet Guide	9
Advertising	10
Announcements	15
Bicycles and the Tube	18
Buying a Ticket	21
Cleaning and Maintenance	25
Directions	31
Drinking on the Tube	33
Eating on the Tube	37
Fashion	40
Fitness and the Tube	43
Games to Play on the Tube	47
History of the Tube	59
Humour	66
Impact on Sanity	70
Insomnia and Tube Travel	72
Judicious Improvements to the Tube	75
Knowledge is a Wonderful Thing	82
Locations	85
London Congestion Charges	88
Lost Luggage	90
Music	94
Naming of Stations	99
Other People on the Tube	104

Pets and the Tube	108
Philosophy	111
Platform Positioning	113
Queens, Kings and 'A' List Celebrities	116
Rage	118
Reading	122
Safety Announcements	126
Science and the Tube	130
Signs	132
'Ten Commandments	136
Time	138
Toilets in London	144
Unanswered Questions	147
Vandalism	149
Weather and Seasons	151
What If?	157
X-rated	163
Yoga's Benefits for Securing Carriage Space	167
Zones	173
Tube Dictionary	175
Conclusion	195

ACKNOWLEDGMENTS

My thanks must go to Transport for London for providing probably the best website of any organisation I know and despite my many observations at their expense, providing a service that by its sheer complexity and the fact that it runs at all, shows what an amazing job they actually do. If you do have some spare time, the website is well worth a visit www.tfl.gov.uk Of course with the extensive use of handheld computers you can always entertain yourself by reading this site while undertaking your daily commute.

INTRODUCTION

Have you ever travelled on an underground train, more affectionately known in London as the Tube? Have you squeezed into the corner of an already packed carriage? Have you wondered what's going on, as the lights in the carriage flicker on and off during your journey, or when you find yourself inexplicably stationary in a tunnel? Have you yearned for a bunged up nose as you are overpowered by the odours along the corridors? Have you started to crave the bag of chips that a fellow passenger is in the middle of eating and been tempted to reach across and take one? If you can answer yes to any of these questions, then I dedicate this book to you, particularly if you answered yes to the bit about the chips.

I have designed this guide to do nothing of any real value. It is here to join you wallowing in the addictive misery that is commuting on the Underground and to help you to gain a deeper insight into your fellow passengers. I have written some parts to make Tube travel more fun and some parts may make it more bearable. However, be warned, opening your eyes to certain aspects of Tube travel, may have the opposite effect and make the whole experience totally unbearable.

I am starting from the assumption that the English, together with the Scots and the Welsh, value their personal space and privacy. We don't greet people with a kiss; we do it at arm's length, with a handshake. We are not by nature a tactile race. A crowded Tube train means putting our 'Britishness' aside, for the duration of the journey, something that is often easier said than done. Despite the Tube being alien to our nature, it is essential. For some perverse reason that escapes my understanding, it is also one of the most fascinating methods of transport and one that most of us, here in Great Britain, at some time in our life, are likely to use.

This book may change your life. By the time you finish reading it, you may want to, a) Change job, if you currently commute by Tube. b) Think differently about your fellow passengers. (In this instance, differently does not equal better.) or c) Book days off work, or even set aside weekends, specifically to spend time travelling on the Tube. And just think about the personal space you will gain from laughing out loud, for no apparent reason. Your fellow passengers may now think that you are completely insane, but look on the bright side, they don't know your name, you may never see them again and you now have a passenger free zone in all directions around you. If this is the case, then I take back the sentence that said this book is of no real value; this would clearly be a RESULT.

This book will not answer the question 'Why take the Tube in the first place?' I have given that question serious thought; sadly, I am no closer to finding the answer. Somewhere deep inside, despite everything I am about to describe, there is a fundamental fascination with travelling in that 'other world' that is the Underground. It brings out the child in everyone. Can you put your hand up and say there isn't a tiny part of you that still believes it might be possible to enter a secret passage, a fantasy world, or a parallel universe, just by going into the Tube? Maybe our addiction is the fascination with science; maybe it is the thought of spending time in somewhere that feels far from reality. On the other hand, maybe, we honestly believe the Tube is the best way to travel. This last explanation does not cover why, from an early age, like it or not, we all want to travel by Tube. The Underground is like a drug with an addictive quality. On the one hand, it repulses you by its necessity and neediness. On the other hand, the Tube thrills you with its sheer scale and its ability to magically carry you from one place to another, in an almost 'time travel' like atmosphere. I stand as an observer to its quirkiness and the impact that it can have on the poor passengers, not all of whom have the time or inclination to admire the sheer magnificence of its creation.

Most travellers achieve a total close-down of the senses, in order to survive travelling by Tube on a regular basis. You may have noticed much of what follows, for yourself, when you were still in your early days of travelling by Tube. If you still notice most of this after the first six months, you will be leading a very unhappy existence and may well be developing a number of unhealthy characteristics.

Please be warned, if you have developed a complete immunity to the worst aspects of Tube travel, then by reading this book you are risking reawakening your senses and making Tube travel, once again, completely unbearable. The author would like to point out that you cannot hold her responsible for this. If you feel strong enough to deal with the risks, read on. Good luck and enjoy the ride.

Lovers take up less space

What's the first thing you think of when you think about lovers? Just for a moment, leave aside the regular tiffs, the broken promises and the rude reality of dirty socks left in the corner of the bedroom. Lovers like to be close together. In a room full of spare chairs, you will find them sitting on the same one. Sometimes in public, they want to be embarrassingly close. They want to be so close in fact that the rest of us feel the need to turn away, except small children who opt to stare at them, until pulled away.

If you're squeamish of such intimacy, the Tube is probably no place for you. Unless of course you are able to overcome your squeamishness and turn the inevitable closeness of Tube travel to your advantage. There is an opportunity, if you can conquer your principles, to obtain more space and make money from encouraging this level of acquaintance to spread to other passengers.

The linchpin of improving your Underground experience is always to encourage friends, neighbours, colleagues, anyone who knows you and for that matter anyone who doesn't, to travel to work with a lover. As long as only some of them choose to travel at the same time as you and some choose to travel at the times that their lover would have been travelling, there should be no net increase in the number of people in your carriage. This reduces the amount of space each travelling pair takes up. It is worth becoming evangelical about this as the first step of your survival strategy.

If 'Plan A' is not working, don't give up. Instead, adopt 'Plan B', which is to start a dating agency in your usual morning carriage. You then need to encourage all non-attached passengers and people who are normally attached to partners they have left at home, to pair off. "Why?" I hear you ask. "Why in Heaven's name," (Ken Livingstone's or Boris Johnson's – or who so ever you choose to invoke) "are you suggesting such excesses?" I can hear you from here and I am, thankfully, nowhere near London. I'm not saying it should be compulsory, at least not initially, but lovers, travelling to work together on the Tube, don't mind being squeezed up against each other. Lovers, unless in the middle of one of their 'tiffs', are unlikely to need any personal space separating them from each other. They choose to squeeze up against each other even when the rest of the carriage is empty. It's great, it leaves more room for the rest of us.

The dating agency may also provide an additional source of income. If the 'lover' is only travelling to be with their partner, this must be discouraged. There will be legislation introduced at a later stage to deal with this, as they are taking up more space than is the single person on his or her own. In these circumstances, encourage passengers to leave their normal partner at home and take another 'essential' traveller as their lover for the duration of the journey.

As a plan, it is foolproof. Lovers don't develop psychopathic tendencies by invading each other's personal space. In the early infatuation stage, they may not even notice whether the other has washed that morning. (A point with regard to Tube travel we will come back to later.) The Tube was designed for lovers. It is an undeniable truth that lovers take up less space than do two passengers travelling separately.

I am assuming that you do not fall into the category of 'people travelling with their lover'. If you're reading this book whilst not on the Tube, I may be wrong about you, but if you are engrossed in reading this while travelling on the Underground, I remain confident in my assumption.

Strange as it may seem to the more romantic among you, there are people who have proposed on the Tube, or who have been proposed to. You may be one of them. Perhaps if that is where you originally met, it is the most romantic place you could choose. A word of advice if you are thinking of proposing on the Tube, take a spare carrier bag to kneel on, you never know what you're going to find on the floor.

At the other extreme, you may have instigated your divorce while travelling by Tube. If you follow up the suggestion of starting a dating agency, you may be the cause of other people instigating divorce proceedings. (It may be worth taking out insurance, as protection against disgruntled spouses, before starting the agency.) I feel safe to assume that, if you are reading this book on the Tube, you are not in the process of meeting the person you will in the future propose to, unless they are looking over your shoulder, trying to read your book, right now. In which case, don't turn round. Staring can put them off. Alternatively, you may in fact be reading someone else's book whilst contemplating nibbling their ear. If they do not know you, this may come as a bit of a surprise, so please explain that it is a direct result of reading this book over their shoulder. I would be quite grateful if you would also explain that the author can in no way be held responsible for your actions. At your age, you should have learnt some self-control.

The lovers may be responsible for some of the Tube's annual complaints about vibrations. Although reading the Transport For London website, I think this is more to do with people complaining about the trains causing vibrations, than it is about the lovers in the carriages causing vibrations to the trains, but you can never be too certain.

So let's go back to the beginning and look at the implications of travelling by Tube from A through to Z...

Alphabet guide

Advertising

There are three types of advertising on the Tube, well four if you include the graffiti and I'm not even going to begin to discuss the things advertised by the graffiti. Firstly, taken from the stance of your arrival at the station, adverts, running the length of the escalators, bombard you, one after another after another after . . . lots of small adverts in frames. Generally, the escalator passes them too quickly to be able to read much in the way of the small print. However, the more sensible advertisers increase your chance of reading them by repeating the posters at intervals along the way. As a rule and this is an aspect of the 'Tubelight Zone', there is always one too few of any particular poster on any escalator journey to read the whole advert, or maybe I need to learn to read faster. You would think that the advertising agencies might have learnt to keep their messages simple enough to take in at one glance, but this is rarely the case. It never ceases to amaze me how out of date some of these posters can be. There is nothing worse than having spent three journeys trying to finish reading the advert for the "Exciting show that has…" "…that has just opened…" "…just opened…and running" "running at the Adelphi . . ." "Adelphi Theatre until…" only to find, on reaching the date, that it has also, sadly, already 'just closed'.

The second type of advertising is on the platforms themselves. These adverts are always the most exciting. The posters use the large available space imaginatively and they can often be quite informative. They also hit me at a time when I rarely have anything better to do than read them. However, I think there should be a law passed to prevent the use of golden beaches and beautiful mountains in such adverts. It is cruel to the poor passenger, when they are stuck below ground, to present them with such images of the world above. Frankly, it's enough to make you turn round and leave the insanity of this other world and for the little voices in your head to be shouting, "Let me out," long before any train approaches. Though having said all of that, I have often wondered whether the lovely people at Transport for London could use technology to project images of the real world onto the brickwork in the tunnels, to stop it feeling so oppressive; maybe images of the streets above would somehow make it more normal. If they put their mind to it, they could make it quite fun. They could project real, or computer simulated, images of looking up through imaginary windows in the roofs of the tunnel at the view, as you would see it from that angle. In the interests of decency, they would have to leave out the people, at least those wearing skirts and dresses. They could then advertise it as a whole new sightseeing experience, "See London from the comfort of the Tube. All the sights without having to leave the train." With the amazing quality of simulation, no one need ever know it wasn't real.

Finally, once you enter the Tube train itself, you are faced with further advertising. I am presuming that the advertising agencies selling the space are doing so based on the audience the adverts are likely to attract. That being the case, I don't understand why the adverts along the escalators are for bookshops, restaurants, shows, exhibitions, alcohol and other interesting products; the ones on the platform are for holiday destinations; and the ones on the trains are all for cheap phone calls, travel insurance and pregnancy advice. Surely, the same audience sees all the adverts. Perhaps they think the people who ride up and down the escalators and stand on the platforms are an entirely different audience from the ones on the trains. Maybe there is some deep psychology that suggests that at different stages of your journey you are ready to absorb different types of messages. Given how long the average commuter spends on the train, unable to move any limbs due to the people around them, they could at least have the decency to make the adverts interesting and change them frequently enough to relieve the boredom. After half an hour, I don't care that I could ring Uruguay for as little as 7p a minute. However, the passengers intimately entwined in the corner may benefit from the pregnancy advice.

I suppose in mentioning four types of advertising, strictly speaking that was not correct. You can read the fifth type of advertising over fellow passengers' shoulders. Here you can continue to discover the delights of London. Apparently, I could buy a two bedroom flat for £340,000 a massive reduction of £60,000 on their previous price. Where I come from, you buy a flat for the price of the reduction and get the whole block for less than the cost of a London penthouse.

A while ago, I became aware of yet another form of advertising on the Tube. This type was even more alarming than all the others and that was fake passengers.

Lovers Take up Less Space

I guess my suggestion of three types of advertising was a little misleading, as this is type number six. Anyway, this type involved the artificial passengers, sitting there, or more likely standing, discussing the merits of a product and how useful they thought that product was. They did this solely as a way to get other people to try it. Advertisers base this on the theory that we are most likely to buy from a trusted source and therefore the recommendation of someone we believe not to be linked to the product is one such source. It is vaguely possible that you will think this is a form of fraud and that you are being duped.

There are many reasons that this type of advertising on the Tube should not be permitted. Primarily, we are all far too gullible and need to be protected from ourselves. Secondly, there are already more than enough people travelling on the Tube and people simply travelling in order to sell to us only make matters worse.

However, it ought to be possible to spot this as a set-up for a number of reasons. Firstly, people don't talk enthusiastically on the Tube, not about anything, never mind the wonders of a new floor cleaner. Secondly, the Tube is not the place you spark up a random conversation about the merits of your washing powder, unless you have just sat in something unpleasant, for which you will need to use it when you get home. Thirdly, even having blanked out the world, you might spot that the same people get on at one station and off at the next then move to the next carriage to repeat the exercise all the way along the train, while all the time discussing the relative merits of something you then feel compelled to rush out and buy.

What is scary is that there are passengers who would

regard complete strangers as a 'trusted source'. However, the same principle applies to the take up rate from items, which people you can't remember, or have never met, but still accepted as friends on social media sites, claim that they 'like'. Like sheep to the truck to market, we see them as people to trust and dutifully follow along.

It's a bit like the time I went to the tyre garage and was offered 'special' air for my tyres at a premium price. The bloke next to me waiting for his car said to me, "You ought to have it. It's much better." I asked him what his authority for this was. It turned out that it was the bloke behind the counter; the one who was selling it. I rest my case.

Announcements

When travelling by Tube there are announcements that will become familiar to you. All too familiar!

"Please mind the gap between the train and the platform." This is regularly shortened to plain and simple "Mind the gap." This announcement seems to be a total cover for the misjudging of distances when building some of the stations. How difficult would it be to get the distance, between the platforms and where the train is supposed to stop, correct? Alternatively, it may be the result of movement of the ground since laying the track, meaning it is no longer as close as it used to be. This would give me greater concern that at some point the whole track wouldn't meet up. The remaining possibility seems to be that the train manufacturers have made trains that ignore the actual size requirements. Perhaps trains went metric and lines stayed in imperial measurements or maybe the manufacturers are seeing it more in terms of making a design statement in preference to issues of practicality. The truth, I believe, is connected with some platforms being slightly curved meaning that at some points the straight train carriage is further away, but then if they had built them straight we would have missed out on a phrase that has become an institution in its own right.

"Please stand clear of the closing doors." This

announcement states the ridiculously obvious. You really don't want to get trapped part in and part out of the train. You don't even want to get stuck with you inside and your bags outside. The gist of the announcement is, "We are about to go so please don't hold us up by getting in the way." I wonder what they said before 1929, when there were still manually operated doors. "Would the last person in please close the door and look lively about it or the person running down the escalator is going to try and get on as well."

"Change here for...," This is standard wording for stations that interchange with either another Tube line, or a mainline rail service. The announcement rarely seems to tell you which mainline rail service. It simply says "Change here for mainline rail services." Unsuspecting travellers could find themselves heading for completely the wrong part of the country.

"Alight here for...," Some places get special treatment and are included in the announcement. The Royal National Institute for the Blind is one such example. Now I can understand why that one is particularly helpful, but as to how Transport for London decides on any other venues that it tells you to alight for, I have no idea. I've often wondered if the opportunity to decide where you can 'alight' is part of someone's job description.

"Please take all your belongings with you when leaving the train." This is not an announcement for your benefit. More to the point any unattended packages left on the Tube present a considerable security risk. The announcement is more of a plea to save the hassle otherwise caused, than a reminder out of concern for you wanting your belongings.

"…This train terminates here." Just in case you were thinking you could go any further, or had forgotten to get off the train, this is a friendly reminder that whether or not this is the stop you thought you wanted, it is the one you've got. It is also a reminder that they do not expect you to move in and make the Tube your home, or for that matter spend all day going backwards and forwards on the same train for the price of a single ticket. Perhaps the tannoy announcement should be changed "…This is the final station. That is unless you have a railcard, have nothing better to do and would like to wait until the train starts its next journey. In which case, … is the first station, please enjoy your ride."

BICYCLES AND THE TUBE

Bicycles are allowed on the Tube, but not at peak times, unless they're the folding ones with tiny wheels that take twice as much pedal power to get anywhere. If you work in the city and want to use a combination of bicycle and Tube you either need to work long hours, short hours or odd hours (start before 07.30 and be home by 16.00 for example) and be prepared to look totally uncool.

However, if you're free to travel outside peak times you must be prepared for a 'stop and start' journey, as bicycles are not allowed on all stretches of the track. (Actually, they aren't allowed on the 'track' at all, as with passengers they need to travel inside the carriages.) If for example you want to get from Edgware to Hampstead, six stops apart on the same Tube line, you can get the Tube for the first two stops. You're allowed to take your bicycle on this stretch. You would then have to get out and cycle for one stop where you could then get back on the train at Hendon Central, only to have to get off two stops later at Golders Green from whence you would have to cycle one stop to Hampstead. What is not clear is why there are odd short lengths of the same journey that you can't take a bike on. It is the same train, on the same line, on the same journey. This would suggest it is not about accessibility. If you can use a station to get on the train to go in one direction, or get off it at that point, surely you can use the same station to get on the train to go in the other direction. Perhaps predicted traveller numbers suggest that certain lengths of track have more passengers and there is therefore likely to be less room for bicycles. Whatever the reasoning, there is nothing like trying to make it easy for the traveller and this is nothing like trying to make it easy.

What would be interesting to find out (and I don't know the answer to this, although I can probably guess) is, are the stretches of road between Underground stations that don't permit bicycles, better served with 'bicycle lanes' on the roads to connect them to the next bike friendly station? "Dear Boris, it has come to my attention…," Just a thought.

In reality, I cannot imagine that anyone would be keen to carry his or her bicycle down to the Tube in the first place. If it is difficult to negotiate an escalator when accompanied by a giraffe (see section on Pets), it is going to be equally difficult with a bicycle in tow. Those with the luxury of lightweight racing bikes might happily sling them over their shoulders and negotiate many obstacles, but with a heavy 'sit up and beg', don't mind getting it nicked, sort of a bike, the prospect is a little less attractive. Perhaps you need to be a stunt rider and nonchalantly cycle your way through the ticket control, with a neat lift over the barrier at just the right moment, followed by remaining on your bike and cycling down the escalator, weaving between the passengers who are standing on the wrong side of the steps.

Even if they do negotiate their way as far as the platform, I cannot imagine, how at any busy time cyclists can 'rush' a carriage to secure space for both themselves and their bikes, without causing serious injury to a number of other passengers. This would be an occasion when steel toe-capped shoes would be useful. If you're going to combine Tube travel with cycling, it looks as though an uncool 'fold-up' bicycle or a unicycle would be your best options.

It is interesting to consider the note on the Los Angeles transit website. Now I realise this is digressing from the immediate vicinity of the Tube, but the same principle is likely to apply where you combine public transport and cycling. Apparently, it is common for people to leave their bikes behind on buses. Picture the scene, you cycle from home to the bus stop and catch your bus. Then you get off the other end and you cycle from the bus stop to the office. On the way home, you cycle from the office to the bus stop and catch the bus. Then you get off, in your cycle helmet, with trousers clipped against all eventualities and you don't manage to notice your bike is missing. There you are going home, with your legs going round and round in thin air where the pedals should be and making absolutely no progress, changing gear has no effect and it's only when ringing your bell to get someone to move out of your way that you finally realise what's missing. You must have left the bell somewhere and perhaps you left the bicycle in the same place.

Buying a ticket

Buying a ticket is a critical aspect of Tube travel. If you've joined a queue at a ticket office, or waited to use one of the automatic machines, only to find it out of order, or not giving change, you'll realise it is not always the easiest thing to achieve.

It never ceases to amaze me how often we will form an orderly queue in front of a broken machine. The first electronic ticket machine was introduced in 1908 and I suspect that some of the queues have been forming ever since. We stand there for any length of time, patiently waiting our turn to buy a ticket. Meanwhile the person at the front of the queue realises the machine is broken and quietly moves away without bothering to tell the rest of the queue. Then the next person does the same and the next and eventually it's your turn and after half an hour of waiting, you find the little 'out of order' sign turned on and no tickets being dispensed. What do you do? You move quietly away and don't tell all the people that are waiting behind you, just like everybody else did.

The only time you get to find out that the ticket machine is broken is when it swallows someone's 20p coin. Then all hell breaks loose and it becomes an urgent mission for them to recover their money. At this point, the queue behind them becomes restless and starts grumbling. Rarely do the people in the queue have the sense to think 'that machine is not working we'd better find somewhere else to pay, rather than stand here and moan'. The British are a nation of 'queuers' and a machine being broken is not seen as good enough reason to stop queuing in front of it.

The great news is, as long as you are not a short-term visitor to the city, Transport for London does what it can to make the process easier. If you travel regularly, you can get a season ticket or an Oyster card to cover all your types of travel. As they have made buying a ticket easier for the Londoners using the Tube, the perception is that the rest of us don't need as many ticket offices with real human beings anymore. If you live outside of London and more especially if you're a foreign visitor, trying to buy a ticket becomes harder to achieve. As a result of the changes to tickets, some staff were able to work shorter hours, the bad news was that the time they didn't work allowed you and me to spend more time in a longer queue for a broken machine, to make up for it.

The principal of 'Oyster' is great as it sets a maximum you can spend on journeys in any one day, but it needs to be simple enough for Non-Londoners to use, know about and not over 'top-up' with credit they will never spend.

'Here's the good news, folks, your total daily journeys will be cheaper than the sum of the individual ones. However, we are very sorry you have a spare £16 on your Oyster card please follow the refund procedure to have it returned. Oh and by the way, there will be an administration charge for the privilege.'

At least the money on an Oyster card doesn't expire. When you visit London, again in three years' time your

Oyster card will still be valid. That is as long as you haven't lost the card at the back of a drawer in the meantime.' The idea also presumes that the system doesn't change in that time. The next thing we're going to hear is that muggers are stopping people for their Oyster cards. Although this has been thought of and you can register and stop them like any other credit card. Alternatively, in the current financial market, Oyster cards may be seen as a safer form of investment than many banks and building societies, even if they don't pay interest. On this basis a small admin fee might be rather less than you might lose on your money elsewhere.

In their advice on using the Underground, Transport for London did, at one point, advise against buying a ticket on a Monday morning. If you plan to travel on a Monday morning and don't live in London then can I suggest your options seem to be somewhat limited. I think what they were really saying was would you mind rearranging your travel to a time of day more convenient to them. This is rather like the call centres where you get a recorded message suggesting you ring back a time when they are less busy, rather than them having to staff to cover the times that their customers actually want to use their services. Who said the customer was king?

At one point Transport for London did publish the list of the top ten queues. (Now there is a potential subject for a whole book about the English.) This list suggested that, based on averages, your best bet if you like queuing was to go to King's Cross where the average was a whole 1.4 minutes worse than the next offender. This was a fact that some of us had suspected for some time, principally in the many wasted minutes standing in the queue at King's Cross, sometimes even on a Monday morning.

How daring! I'm guessing some of this was due to the work for St Pancras's International hub and once work around that area completed those queues probably reduced, although with the arrival of many foreign travellers, this may have an equal and opposite effect.

To confuse travellers using travel passes in New York, following a strike on the network, travel pass holders were asked to 'manually' calculate the appropriate extension to their cards for the three strike days. This was because the electronic computerised 'card readers' were unable to figure this out without assistance and presumably could not be reprogrammed at an overall level. If you bought a seven-day pass, for a week's holiday and found the strike had affected three days, you might have been a 'little' disappointed. What I couldn't work out was how travellers managed to get through the barriers. When the 'card reader' refused their passes for being out of date, were they able to say to the 'card reader' "That's ok it's still valid. Don't forget the strike days." At which point the 'card reader' might reply, "Oh, of course, silly me, whatever was I thinking. Have a nice day". Such behaviour may sound odd, but I do know people who say "Thank you," aloud, without thought of embarrassment, to car park ticket machines when their little displays come up with messages like "Have a safe journey".

Cleaning and maintenance

Regular travellers will appreciate that cleaning in and around the Tube has to be one of the worst jobs imaginable. All those who give their lives to this thankless, but noble, cause should receive a knighthood as a right after five years of service.

You hear announcements over the tannoy –"Would a cleaner please go to point X, where they have a Code 10". You listen to these announcements or ones similar and wonder what the code means. If you are standing at point X and know someone has just been sick, urinated, left a used needle or whichever other dreadful thing they have done, you may then discover the meaning of the code; if not, you remain in blissful ignorance.

As a passenger, I am grateful for the use of codes, because there are some occasions when I really wouldn't cope too well with hearing "Would a cleaner please go urgently to platform 2, where some despicable yob has just vomited last night's drinking spree, together with the curry he ate earlier." Then when I think about it, just hearing a code I start imagining the possibilities. Do they have a code for the discovery of body parts, or whole passengers who another passenger has murdered for eating chips and bacon sandwiches without passing them round?

Are staff at times tempted to use the codes as a way of dealing with normal communication? What for example is the code for, "Jim, your tea's ready"? Is there a code for "Some halfwit has spray painted his initials over the sign for the Bakerloo line, again"? Maybe there's a code that means "Scantily clad, very attractive, blond on platform 3". These are questions that face poor passengers every day. After a while, you stop hearing these voices, which are, mysteriously, always so much clearer than those relating to the train announcements which ARE relevant to passengers.

Passengers stop seeing so many things, such as the graffiti and then they stop smelling the smells. For me, sadly, that last point has never happened. I have never managed to stop smelling the smells. Travelling by Tube is the more unpleasant for having a well-developed sense of smell. Oh, the glorious times when you are so bunged up with cold that you can't smell anything, although at these times commuting is unpleasant for a multitude of other reasons.

I have learnt the points where it is generally better to hold my breath, to avoid the smell. Unfortunately, I have never been able to hold my breath for any great length of time. I even practise holding my breath when outside of London. If you want to try this, I highly recommend lines of bus stops used by drunken revellers. I find these bus stops are an ideal location to try walking past without inhaling a breath. Despite the practise, sadly, I am still not that good at it. However, short of discovering a way to hold my breath the entire time I am below ground, or resorting to wearing scuba diving equipment, with large oxygen cylinders, I suppose I'll have to put up with a certain amount of the smell whilst travelling by Tube.

Lovers Take up Less Space

I have considered carrying oxygen cylinders as a key survival technique. As yet, I have not devised a way of getting sufficient space in rush hours to get my oxygen cylinders onto the train. The best I have come up with is to disguise the oxygen cylinders as a rucksack and pretend to be a student. I might still find the mask over the face would give it away. Then how long would it be before I was mugged for my oxygen? This does not appear such a bright idea when you think of the risks.

You can understand why they don't make Tube carriages more like aeroplanes, with the oxygen masks that fall down from the ceilings in the event of an emergency. You can just imagine them being vandalised by desperate passengers eager to breathe fresh air. Wartime gas masks might be a more discreet solution. However, whilst these would be a great boost for Army & Navy Store sales, this might also serve to heighten the anxiety levels in more nervous passengers, who might presume the motivation to be more sinister.

There are a number of ways that Transport for London could improve the Tube by copying other transport systems. When you land by plane in some countries, they spray the cabin with some unidentifiable substance to kill bugs, rather than let them enter their countries. I would like to advocate this for Tube journeys. I spend too long wondering what creatures and germs I am sharing the carriage with as a result of my fellow passengers. Little toilet cubicles stocked with nice soaps and hand creams would be appreciated. Maybe this would only be in the first class carriages of the Brave New Tube World. After all, they are non-existent on planes after the first ten minutes of the journey, once the fasten seat-belt light goes out.

I find it quite bizarre that there is a little plaque with the date of refurbishment shown in the carriage. If the renewal programme was to a very short timescale and they were trying to impress passengers with just how recently they had refurbished the carriage, this might be understandable. But to find I am sitting (if I'm lucky) amidst fifteen years of accumulated debris and heaven only knows what, simply increases the tendency of my imagination to run away from me. At which point in that fifteen years did, for example, a drunken reveller scratch his initials on the ceiling and how did he reach? Was he seven feet tall or did he stand on something?

Still, none of this is as bad as sitting down and after a while starting to get the sensation that the seat is damp. If you're lucky, that will be because whatever problem there was, has been washed out of the seat and it is still wet from washing. The chances of that are fairly low, but it's advisable to hold that thought. If you let your mind wander to other possible causes, it will pass spilt drink quite quickly on its way to something much worse. You still have to deal with, 'when I stand up, is there going to be a mark on my trousers?' and 'is my coat long enough to cover it'? This will in turn lead to some very bizarre walking patterns, as you try to see your rear end in shop windows, or anything that will act as a mirror. What is certain is that when you get home that particular garment will be going straight into the washing machine – or, depending on how bad the situation is, the bin!

It is worth including in your survival pack a change of clothing, just to be on the safe side. And all to get between Piccadilly and Leicester Square.

Now I know I have a vivid imagination, but there are two additional thoughts that I've had at intervals. Firstly, do the sewage pipes go above or below the underground tunnels? All things being equal, this should not make any difference. However, what if there was a leak? Is this in itself a reason not to use the deeper Tube lines? What code of situation would that be, in being declared over the tannoy?

Secondly and much along the same lines, do you ever wonder in passing under the River Thames, whether the structures above are strong enough to support that volume of water? Now, I'm no scriptwriter, but what a film plot that would make. An Underground train, stuck in a tunnel under the river, when it floods. Oh, there would be a horror film to compete with the best. This would not be a question of how long before you dare go back in the water, more how long before you dare go by Underground under the water. I think that as a film it would be a good investment for the 'above water' river crossing companies to fund the filming. It would do wonders for the trade of water taxis. Alternatively, maybe someone could invent a 'submarine-train'. There are cars that can go on land and in water, why not trains?

There is currently a fantastic programme to modernise the Tube and the stations that serve it. This has led to the upgrade of many stations, the introduction of air conditioning where possible and making the Underground fit for the 21st century. However, it seems an unfortunate turn of phrase in a press release about making a station 'state of the art' to have described it as a 'concrete example' of the investment (10 Feb 2005). I now picture a brand new grey 'concrete' mass rather than the gleaming glass and steel that 'state of the art' brought to mind.

When it comes to maintenance you have to wonder

quite what is going on when you find some of the American Subway companies selling off 'surplus' items. If you look on the Internet, you can find them advertising escalator parts. Do you think the ones they were selling were escalators that had been finished with? Perhaps they were just dismantling one that should be in use, for the fun of it. Sometimes the train companies go even further and whole carriages are retired. One moved to take up a new position as a studio, for hospital radio, at Great Ormond Street Hospital. They had to use an articulated lorry and a crane to get it there. What I couldn't work out is how they got it up the escalator to get it to street level in the first place.

Interestingly, within the Tube's 'Environmental Report', I can find no mention of targets to reduce the number of people urinating in inappropriate places. Without this, there is little hope of any serious improvement to the environment of the Underground.

Directions

When leaving a platform you will often see signs saying, "This side up" and "No entry". Through experience and curiosity, I have reached the following conclusions.

1) The direction that is signposted is always the longest way round.

2) If you go up the side that people are coming down you will cause them maximum annoyance.

Correct timing of going up the "No Entry" side i.e. when no one is coming the other way, will shorten the time it takes to get out. Please don't be fooled. You start out going up a 'no-entry' thinking there is no one coming, when as a result of a train arriving at another platform, you suddenly get caught in the stampede of people coming towards you. In these situations, it is wise to remember, you are the one that's normal. It's all of them that are odd. Of course, given that going out of a 'no exit' or in a 'no entry' directly contravenes the byelaws. I cannot condone this behaviour and I know none of this from personal experience.

Although I cannot support breaking rules, I challenge you to find a single passenger who has never contravened the extensive byelaws. These specifically prohibit everything from trying to get on to a train before the passengers getting off have done so, to trying to get on to a train when the doors have started to close and that's all before you come to the rules about it being forbidden to be intoxicated on the Tube. By this time, I can't imagine many of you are feeling so self-righteous.

As for directions on the platform itself – see the section on Signs and don't expect to find yourself any the wiser, particularly of course if your first language is not English.

DRINKING ON THE TUBE

Some of the things you see as you travel round London look very out of place. They aren't the sort of things that you're brought up to expect. I realise this probably reflects a sheltered upbringing and a level of prejudice which I wasn't aware of until now, but I hadn't thought of tramps appreciating the finer things in life.

You never know the sad state of affairs that has led to people making the streets their home. I presume for the most part it is not their first choice of accommodation. Many of them may once have lived with the finer things every day. Most of them are bright intelligent people. For example, I have noticed that there are proportionately more people without homes choosing to sleep out in the warmer, drier part of this and other countries, than in the colder damper parts. They have deliberately not chosen, for example, to live in the wetter city of Manchester and before the lovely Mancunian people lambast my analogy, you have, in fairness, chosen to live indoors.

Despite all of this, I was still surprised by one particular occasion. A group of what I presumed were homeless people, unless they were lost commuters, sitting around Charing Cross station, wrapped in blankets, looking to have absolutely nothing to their names. Let's face it if you weren't homeless, Charing Cross is not likely to be your first choice of seating. However, it should be noted that they seemed happy, which is more than can be said for most of my fellow Tube travellers. As I walked along, heading for a packed carriage, on an over-warm train, another person came and joined their number. He was carrying paper cups and a bottle. That in itself did not strike me as unusual. There are many on the streets who find solace in a cheap bottle of alcohol, quite apart from the commuters. What struck me on this occasion was when he gently popped the Champagne cork and poured the 'bubbly' out for his compatriots. I guess we all have times we want to celebrate. Who says that if you're down on your luck it means you stop having better moments to toast and a taste for the good life? They may of course have been celebrating no longer having to commute, an event I would happily raise a glass to, or a paper cup as appropriate. It may have been that they had secured a bed for the night or it may have been that the person who gave them the money was in banking, had just received a large bonus payment and was making a down-payment on a future pitch, in case his luck changed and the need arose.

The Tube makes you share an intimate space with many you wouldn't allow to get that close in other circumstances. Take the scruffy drunken bloke on the platform at Shepherd's Bush. There I stood minding my own business, when I heard him ask, "Which way do I go to Finsbury Park?" To be precise it was more "Wish wayyyyyyy Fnsbrrrrrrrrry Paaaaaaaark?" Much as I was tempted to use that old classic, "Well I wouldn't start from here," I realised he was far too drunk to get the joke. As it turned out, I didn't know the way to Finsbury Park or probably for that matter any other park in London, so I said I couldn't help. The man standing next to me told him he'd need to change at King's Cross, for the Northern line and the drunk wobbled a yard or two away. Shortly afterwards, when he had wobbled back in my direction, there was an announcement that there were problems on the Circle Line and trains would be stopping at Baker Street. Attempting rather feebly to be the Good Samaritan, I thought I was being helpful, pointing out to the drunk that this now meant that the train would not be going as far as King's Cross and he would need to find a different route.

Moral No. 1 - never be helpful to a drunk.

He got onto the Tube and asked for directions from someone else. A passenger who hadn't heard the announcement or didn't much care to give a lengthy explanation to the drunk and who told him to change at King's Cross. The drunk then slurred that it was a good job that some people were helpful and spent the train journey glaring at me. That continued until we all got off at Baker Street, whereas I hurriedly disappeared into the crowd it was hard to resist the burning urge to shout back to him "Don't say I didn't try to tell you." But then, moral number two came to mind.

Moral No 2 - don't antagonise a drunk.

Drinking (of the alcoholic variety) and the Tube do not necessarily mix. Firstly, with alcohol, you will need to squeeze past the byelaw that says 'No person in a state of intoxication shall enter or remain on the railway', which would otherwise eliminate about 75% of those using the Tube in an evening, 90% of those using it in December and 95% on big match-days. Secondly, you still have to contend with the major hazards that the Tube can pose. It seems that for those under the influence of alcohol, the greatest danger is the escalator. This danger is recognised to such an extent that in May 2005, Transport for London ran a 'Tipple but don't Topple' campaign with the posters being strategically placed in bars around Canary Wharf where, in one year, there were 37 escalator accidents, many caused by combining escalators with alcohol. As to why the problem is greater in Canary Wharf I will leave to your imagination, although it may just be that those who travel to and from Canary Wharf are more likely to sue in the event of an accident occurring.

Given the odd venues that people use for 'launch parties' of one sort or another, perhaps the Tube should 'jump on the bandwagon' and hire carriages out for private functions. In this way a few select guests of your choice could lurch their way around the Circle Line, several times, clinking glasses of wine to while away the evening. The entertainment could include watching real commuters trying to cram into even fewer carriages and of course trying to negotiate the escalator at the end of the evening.

Perhaps there is a reason that the Tube doesn't have a licensed buffet car on any of its trains!

Eating on the Tube

The Underground is no place to throw a blanket wantonly on the ground and unpack your picnic. If the sight of rats running along the rails hasn't put you off, then looking at the chewing gum stuck to the bottoms of the seats will. If you are sensitive to matters of hygiene then the Tube is not the first place you would choose for a meal, but there are passengers who see it differently.

During my time commuting, there were people who, as normal practice, would have their breakfast on the Tube. That is not to say that they took a bowl, some Corn Flakes and a pint of milk onto the train, or even a more restrained banana and pot of yoghurt. It was for places such as this that the cereal bar was invented, for people on the move, literally.

Many regular travellers have become adept at getting onto a Tube with a coffee from a drinks stand and a cereal bar of one sort or another. I never got the hang of how this was possible in a crowded train, even without thinking about the number of germs surrounding me, or the repellent smells that make eating less than enjoyable. How do you, whilst carrying scalding coffee, force your way into a 'full' carriage? I'm not saying it's a lesson I want to learn, but having not mastered getting into a full carriage 'empty handed' I can't begin to contemplate how you do it with a rucksack or briefcase, a cereal bar and a scalding hot cup of coffee. I would take my hat off to them, but I'm afraid there isn't enough space to get my arm from by my side and up towards the brim.

Assuming that we don't outlaw eating on the Tube altogether, there are acceptable eating habits and then there are wholly unacceptable ones. There are passengers for whom this distinction does not seem to be clear. To simplify it I have provided some general rules to make it easier for you to gauge the difference.

It is acceptable to eat food that does not smell, is not wet, is not hot and at such times that the train is not so full as to cause the resulting crumbs to fall down your neighbouring passenger's cleavage. Some readers may think eating should fall under the "Games" section of this book with the cleavage being the object of the game. Can I assure you that this behaviour is not consistent with leaving the carriage with the telephone number of the lady concerned, although it might get you that of her lawyer, particularly if the substance dropped were also hot.

On a relatively empty train, you may modify some of these rules. For example, it is permissible to eat a bag of chips on the understanding that you invite the other passengers in the carriage to share them. Otherwise, your fellow passengers may consider carrying chips on a Tube train is mental cruelty. You cannot then hold them responsible for their actions. In these circumstances, actions may vary from pinching a chip uninvited, at one end of the spectrum, to mugging you for the whole bag if very hungry, at the other extreme. You must always offer a ketchup laden bacon sandwich to me, if I am in the carriage (preferably, before you have taken a bite).

Lovers Take up Less Space

If you ignore the advice that the Tube is not the place for a picnic, it is polite to ensure that you bring enough paper plates for all passengers in the carriage and enough food to go on them. This is not the sort of meal that will turn out like 'the feeding of the five thousand', five fish and two loaves only works between people who are concerned about their neighbours and who are predisposed to ensure there will be enough to go round. It is safe on a Tube train to assume that this would need to be the per person quota.

As a survival tactic, it is always worth carrying a large supply of food and drink to keep you going through delays and long journeys, or you can use them as negotiation opportunities in difficult situations. More enticing food will of course work better for this latter purpose, however a three day old, ketchup laden, bacon sandwich, drawn from the depths of your pocket may not, when the chips are down (so to speak), prove quite so effective as a fresh one. On the other hand, eating garlic before you travel may assist you in gaining extra space.

Another trick is to carry a packet of the exceedingly strong mints to offer in the event you find yourself pressed too close to a passenger with bad breath. It has the double benefit of countering their natural odours if they eat one and temporarily overwhelming your sense of smell if you eat one yourself. This is what is called a win:win scenario.

Fashion

When I started working in London, I looked different. I looked like a visitor. I lived one hundred miles away, but in terms of what I wore, it could have been several thousand miles. It was obvious I was not local. The careful advice of a friend soon pulled me into shape. Mysteriously, the friend concerned left London and moved to live in the Caribbean, which is about as far from Tube travel as you can get. However, the survival skills she taught me were invaluable. In an attempt not to be the one to be mugged, look like the people around you, the scruffy people, not the well off ones. I kept my old, threadbare, winter coat that needed throwing out years ago. (At least I told myself that was the reason I kept it. The fact that I still had it in the first place and still have it, may just mean I'm no good at throwing things out.) I wore my old black shoes. They may have leaked, but at least I blended in. Then there's the handbag. Now I'm sorry if this offends anyone, but I've always thought that large shoulder bags, which hold everything from a purse to an A4 file, look cheap. It's the sort of thing that students carry and people who don't have better taste. As a result of working in London, I now have to take it all back, that only applies outside London. I now understand that this kind of bag is perfect to hold everything and hold to your body on crowded Tubes and streets, to reduce the chance of having it snatched. Bag snatching and pick pocketing, or picking pockets as the case may be, have to be the most common crimes in such enclosed spaces, with everyone pushed up against each other. That is likely to remain the case, until failing to wash before using the Tube is made a crime, which despite my lobbying doesn't seem to be entering the statute book any time soon.

After six weeks, I was already insidiously becoming part of this anonymysing process and slowly developing the psychopathic tendencies to go with it. If you want to avoid someone mugging you then think like a mugger. There is a very fine dividing line between the exact amount you should think like a mugger and remaining 'law-abiding'. Don't look vulnerable, don't look different and don't look like you've got anything worth taking. In my case, I didn't have anything worth taking, but this is one of those times that perception becomes reality. If you look like you have something, you are at risk of someone wanting to find out if you really have. Alternatively, you could try looking like a mugger, but this may lead to the unnecessary complications of trips to the police station to 'assist with enquiries'. When you think about who you might be at risk from, don't forget the lovers in the corner. What a perfect disguise. Who would expect that they are arch-criminals mugging unsuspecting passengers in between kisses?

The result of wearing clothes that made me blend in, meant that I, like many around me, could be dressed straight from a charity shop and in fact many are. There was an elderly bloke the other day; he was probably around 80 years old, very shaky on his feet and slumped into a seat, with his hand shaking on the armrest. He was wearing an old tatty shirt with palm trees, with an overlarge collar, an ancient looking coat and a very good pair of… leather trousers. I did a double take and spent the rest of the journey trying to decide which group he fell into. Had he been kitted out by a charity shop? Did he have a leather fetish, which had not reduced with age? Was his motorbike waiting, just outside his Tube stop, to finish his journey home with a bit more excitement? Maybe he did have psychopathic tendencies and switched between Jekyll and Hyde personalities with one as a doddery old man and the other as a serious rock 'n' roll biker.

Then there was the man foppishly flicking his hair, wearing a cream, creased linen jacket and talking too loudly into his mobile phone. He just had to be an art or antique dealer and he so had to be English.

There are many 'dos' and don'ts' of Tube clothing. I have elsewhere explained why it's inadvisable to wear a circular skirt, but it can be plain dangerous to wear trousers that are so long that they, or at least their frayed edges, can add you to the list of 'escalator casualties'. You will also be lucky to find enough space in the carriage in rush hour for any clothes with big padded shoulders, or for that matter any design that takes up additional space. Although, having suitably padded clothing may prevent other passengers from bruising you as easily with their elbows. It is always advisable to wear shoes with steel toecaps. This will both prevent the pain when another passenger treads on you and in the event that you need to retaliate, will leave you perfectly placed.

Whatever else you wear, don't forget you can buy Underground boxer shorts and socks for the London Transport Museum shop.

Fitness and the Tube

Transport for London goes to great lengths to explain how to obtain assistance when travelling and unless you are a six limbed, swivel headed person with the strength and fitness of a prize winning boxer and the physique of a sprite, I suggest that assistance would be beneficial.

Not all stations have lifts or working elevators to the platforms and even those that do, seem to have stairs between the platforms just to confuse the issue. Two hands are not enough to put a ticket in the barrier, carry your luggage and negotiate the exit. In fact, it is my considered opinion that the Tube was designed for use by aliens with at least two good legs and feet and at least four good hands. The arms of these hands should be at varying lengths to enable one to reach the ticket machine slot, one to hold the overhead wrist supports, one or more to carry luggage without getting in the way and one to prod snotty nosed kids out of the way when necessary. I take my hat off to anyone successfully negotiating the Tube with fewer than this number of workable limbs.

What do you do if you want to travel between two points that don't have wheelchair access? At least all the new stations have this covered, but my admiration goes to anyone who is not put off by the fact that they have to get off at a stop five stations along from the one they really want, because it's the nearest one that is accessible.

The odds of Tube travel are firmly stacked in favour of the fit and strong. That would be the nimble, agile, flexible, yoga practising and determined, fit and strong to be precise.

It isn't just those with wheelchairs that must find it difficult. The same problem is true for parents with pushchairs or prams. In theory there is, at least in that situation, one able bodied adult to negotiate the escalator. It's amazing how a cute child always seems to attract more assistance than an adult in need of help. Of course, a screaming child is unlikely to help in this matter, but it will provide the additional all-important space to enable the parent to breathe while standing in the carriage. However, a parent travelling as the lone adult with more than one child is outnumbered before they even begin to contend with a fold down buggy that has lost its ability to fold and an escalator that may or may not be working. You can at least use the buggy as a weapon to fight off other passengers on entering the carriage. You will however, have completely misplaced any small children who you last saw clinging to the bottom of your coat. To make a success of this strategy, you will need the children to wear roller skates and to have tied them tightly to the coat.

The elderly, the infirm, the non-able bodied and the diffident are simply bulldozed out of the way by the more determined passengers. As for anyone who is elderly, infirm, non-able bodied and diffident and who tries to use the Tube, well you're braver than me.

What is the solution? In this instance, I do not think you can entirely solve the problem by finding a suitable lover in the carriage, not least because the problems begin long before you get below ground. Of course, this approach may make the whole experience more bearable, but it isn't necessarily the solution. As far as I can see, we should allow or even encourage all less able bodied or minded travellers whether through medical condition, age, or simply nervousness to adopt suitable survival tactics. I haven't quite devised a way of wheelchairs successfully negotiating stairs and escalators, but I do think they should come with suitable weaponry to enable them to get through. They could have little arms that come out low down to 'nip' the ankles of passengers who stubbornly get in the way, or even fronts a bit like snow ploughs to shovel people aside. There could also be additional arms to deal with the ticket machine and barrier and to pinch peoples' 'rear ends' on trains, on the grounds that no one is going to suspect it was them. Perhaps trains should come equipped with little ramps that extend out to the platform to cover 'the gap', a device that would be just as useful for young girls in tight skirts and high heels as for the less able bodied members of society, or would this spoil the most famous announcement coined by the Tube?

I am aware of instances when travellers, who are able bodied and fit, have feigned illness when travelling in order to obtain assistance. In the instance of some mainline railway travellers, I have heard of times when they have used this as a method of obtaining a cab home at the expense of the train company. Whilst, of course, I deplore such behaviour, there is a small part of me that can't help but wish that I had been born with the ability to carry off such a level of cheek without giving the game away. I was born more of the variety and upbringing that struggles on, pretending everything is fine when it isn't, rather than the getting away with murder variety. During many a Tube journey, I have had time to daydream about what it might be like to carry off acts of bare faced cheek, but I have never got past the dreaming stage.

Games to Play on the Tube

There are many games to play on the Tube. Some passengers will content themselves with the ones on their mobile phone, but here I am offering a number of games specifically designed for the Tube. These games split into ones to pass the time on an otherwise necessary journey and games that are themselves the whole point of the journey. All of these games can form part of your essential survival strategy. There are games you can play in your own head, by observing your fellow passengers or letting your imagination run riot, but the games that follow are of the competitive variety that involve other players as well as yourself. Be warned, in some instances the particular pieces required for the game may lead you to switch to a bigger rucksack.

Travelling with a lover counts as a game in its own right and therefore makes the following section superfluous. The type of games played with your lover should not involve other passengers in addition to the two of you. In the event that you are pursuing this type of play, you may instead need someone on standby to bail you out when you are arrested. The explanation, 'We didn't mean any harm officer. We were only killing time on an otherwise difficult journey. We haven't met before and promise never to do it again,' may be sufficient to resolve the issue, particularly if the officers concerned are regular Tube travellers and have themselves sort ways to pass the time.

These are the games that I have devised for those of you who have not found someone else in the carriage with whom to pass the journey in a warm embrace:

Tube Buy-to-Let – This and the two games that follow have a similar theme. For this one, you will need an official Monopoly set. (This must be the traditional London version, as attempting to play with a Paris or Madrid board will lead to considerable confusion.) You will also need a London A-Z, a railcard for the number of zones covering all Monopoly properties, a digital camera for each player, plenty of time, money for food and drink or a packed lunch. It may also be useful to carry a copy of Tim Moore's book, "Do Not Pass Go" about the game of Monopoly, as a reference guide on where some of the locations can be found.

Having agreed, with your fellow players, on an appropriate pub as an end point, shuffle all the property cards from the game and deal them evenly among the players. The aim of the game is then to travel around London using only the Tube (or foot) to visit and photograph the properties that you have been dealt, before hot footing (or Tubing) it to the agreed end point. The winner is the first one to arrive with a full set of photographs of the locations for which they were dealt the corresponding cards. (These photographs must be on your digital camera with the appropriate time and date mark. Taking a series of photographs of all the Monopoly board locations in advance and then quickly deleting the unnecessary ones is CHEATING!) The only play that can possibly beat a competitor that has legitimately photographed all his properties and returned to the pub, is to find legal, valid and honest 'free parking' within the Congestion Charge Zone, which if proven makes the player an instant winner and a hit with all the other people in the end point bar.

You should note that the 'Community Chest' and 'Chance' cards do not come into play in this game and visits to prison, due to actions taken to win, are entirely at the risk of the player and the author takes no responsibility for these. Any instruction by an officer of the law to "Go to jail, go directly to jail," should be taken seriously as laughing at a police officer on the misunderstanding that it is part of the game, may not be taken well. However, you may want to question why you aren't receiving a fair hearing first. May I remind players that in real life "getting out of jail free" is fictional and unlikely to happen, unless you have completed the relevant term of your sentence. When passing the original start point station, on the way to another destination, it is highly unlikely that anyone will present you with £200 for no reason. Be wary if someone does give you money for no reason, it may be linked to criminal activity and may land the recipient in one of the aforementioned prisons.

Tube Detective – Once again, the theme of the game is travel by Tube around London. You will need an official traditional Cluedo game set, a digital camera for each player, a railcard covering the agreed number of zones and an imagination. A London A-Z is not required but may come in useful when you get lost. A Yellow Pages or London Telephone Directory may also come in handy.

Having agreed a suitable end point with your fellow players, the game can begin. This game takes much less time to play (for most people) than Tube Buy-to-Let. It is cruel to invite friends with no imagination to play and can lead to them tramping round London for several days. Separately, shuffle the people, location and implement cards and as in the real game, draw one from each set. All players then get to see the three cards. This is a complete departure from the board game and if you are someone who is hidebound by rules, you may find this difficult.

The aim of the game is to travel around London to find locations, signs, or any implement that suitably represents the appropriate card. For example, if the Library were the scene of the crime, a photograph of a London library would be in order. Mrs White might be the proprietor of White's Lighting Shop (I've just made that up – there may not be one). Most of the implements can be found in their actual original state in shops and venues around London and if you have a really unlucky day, on the Tube itself. If you live in London, agree a zone of play away from your normal area, to provide a level playing field for all players. Alternatively, lie to your fellow players about which areas you know, in order to give yourself a head start and win the game. Once all players arrive at the pub, you can repeat this game from the start, allowing you to combine the game with a pub-crawl.

Tube Treasure Hunt – This involves wandering aimlessly round London using only the Tube and foot for transport. You will need, a List of treasure, a bag or rucksack, a digital camera, a railcard, a London A-Z for when you get lost, an agreed end point. It is also wise to have an agreed spending limit. This last point is important, as in London you can buy most things for a price! The lower the spending limit the longer the game will take to play.

You should apply a time limit when playing this

game, to prevent 'more determined players' from playing for too long. The aim of the game is to collect the items listed (or photographs of the items) and then return with them, or their photographs, to the end point by the agreed finish time. The winner is the player who arrives with the most items from the list. Award points for each item successfully collected and deduct them for every 15 minutes over the agreed time that it takes for the player to return. Bonus points are available for imagination and sheer nerve. For example if asked to bring back a photograph of yourself with a famous person, you might award 1 point for a photo of you with a cardboard cut out. 2 points for you with a 'look-alike', 3 points for a photo with a real famous person and 5 points if you bring the famous person back to the pub. Please award a bonus of 50 points if the famous person is Matthew Perry and you send him in the direction of the Author.

Suggested items to get your list going are: 1) A photograph of you with a famous person. 2) A Sock. 3) A bus ticket (remember you are only allowed to travel by Tube). 4) 5 Euros. 5) The Crown Jewels (be careful with this one, arrest equals automatic disqualification). 6) The London Eye (you may need a large rucksack). 7) A person who smokes a pipe (remember to ask their permission before taking them back to the pub and the permission of anyone they were travelling with if you leave them behind). 8) A newspaper from yesterday. (Please check no one is sleeping under it before taking. If they are only reading the paper this is not a problem, although courtesy dictates you should give them today's paper as a substitute.) 9) A bar of chocolate (points will be deducted for nibbled corners or pieces missing). 10) A hot bacon sandwich. (You must deduct points for dripping ketchup on route, or if the sandwich has been allowed to go cold. This is easily solved by choosing a pub that you know sells hot bacon sandwiches, as the end point.) 11) A Christmas tree. 12) Hyde Park Corner. 13) A toilet closed sign (These are usually plentiful. A sign which previously said 'To Let', on which you have painted the 'i' and the word closed, does not count.) 14) A sombrero. 15) A pigeon. 16) Some lovers from the Tube. – You get the general idea. To make it more interesting a minimum number of items should be the real thing and not photographs – this is where the spending limit comes in. Of course bribing a person who smokes a pipe to go with you to the pub may be more successful if you don't make them traipse round London looking for other treasure first and if you offer to buy them a pint. Good Luck.

Underground Snap – You can play this game in a number of ways to keep you amused on a journey. Depending on the length of the journey, you might be able to try all the variations listed here on the same trip. Feel free to introduce your own varieties. Award yourself one point for every matching pair of a) adverts b) people c) handbags d) designer labels e) glasses f) tattoos g) hairstyles h) newspapers I) lovers (remember they must be matching) j) bacon sandwiches (matching would be ketchup to ketchup not ketchup to brown sauce. That is a very important distinction to make.) Etc. Record your high score for a particular journey and try to beat it next time you travel. You can achieve much hilarity by inviting your fellow passengers to join in the game, although in this circumstance you run the risk of not leaving your journey with the satisfaction of having won. You may also cause offence to fellow passengers if you tell them you are scoring a point for matching odd shaped noses and it happens to be theirs that provides the point.

Tube Backgammon – In the same way as playing the board game, if someone standing on his or her own takes the space you want, simply tap him or her out of the way and send them back to the start of their journey. Please do this carefully and away from the tracks, as no injury should befall fellow passengers as a result of your game. You can repeat this any number of times until you reach your destination or someone escorts you off the premises, whichever occurs sooner. The biggest danger however is that a fellow travelling passenger is also playing the game and does this to you. In which case there is a risk that you will never arrive at your intended destination. Again, as in the board game, standing with someone else protects you from an opposing passenger performing this action on you. Travelling in packs is the safest option, but makes it unlikely that you will be playing this game at the same time.

Tube Anagrams - Take the first eight letters of the station name and rearrange them to make as long a word as possible. For short station names, such as Bank, use sufficient letters from the word 'station' in order to give eight letters, so for this example b,a,n,k,s,t,a,t . Give yourself points for the number of letters you use. Allow yourself to triple a particular score if you have a seat and to double your score if you are relatively comfortable. You only score the number of letters used if you're standing squashed into a corner.

As with 'Snap' keep a record of your high scores for any particular journey and try to beat it next time. You should not tolerate cheating by allowing yourself double, when squashed between a former well developed shot putter and a snotty nosed kid. Score double for the first three letters of the word if no one sneezes on you during that stretch of the journey and triple the first four letters if someone offers you a chip, but only if it is from a fresh batch and not one that the person has picked up off the carriage floor.

You can devise other scoring systems to suit your level of boredom.

Charades – Watch the people the other side of the carriage. Observe their arm movements (if there is space for arm movements), their body language and if possible lip-read. Try to guess what they are talking about. You should award points for imagination and extra points are award for correct answers. However, in order to find out if you are correct you will need to have the courage to ask them if you were right. I do not recommend this latter course of action. In extreme circumstances, it can lead to them causing you harm, particularly if your guess was wildly inaccurate, or if in fact you correctly guess that they were planning to rob the bank on the corner by the next Tube stop. This is generally not something they will want broadcast.

Going Nowhere Fast – The name of the game speaks for itself. The aim is to work your way around your route to your final destination, before your 'friends' send you home. You will need 1) All day 2) An all zones rail card (a card covering fewer zones may be used depending on the agreed route) 3) An agreed route including start and end point 4) Some dice (one for each player) 5) Some friends. If you are playing this game as part of an existing journey, please continue. However, if you are thinking of playing this game just for fun and didn't need to use the Tube, you might be better advised to buy a board game from the local toyshop, put the coffee on and settle down in the comfort of the sofa.

All players start from the same starting point and take turns simultaneously on the quarter hour. For this purpose, it is wise to set watches to exactly the same time, as you cannot always rely on station clocks within the same station, let alone between competing stations.

Start the game by first agreeing the direction of travel. On rolling the dice all players then travel the number of stops shown on the die that he or she has individually rolled. The player must then leave the train and wait for the next quarter hour to arrive. A degree of trust between players is essential. If a player has been fortunate enough to throw a high number (or the train has been held up) and the quarter hour point occurred during the previous turn, then the next turn should be taken immediately upon alighting from the train onto the platform. Roll the die and catch the next train for the appropriate number of stops. If a player waiting on a platform is joined by a subsequent player, then the first player to arrive is bounced and has to return to the start of the game. You can drop this rule when playing the short version. The pattern of play continues until players are within six stops or fewer of the home station, or agreed end point if a circular route is not being followed. At this point only rolls of the die of numbers equal to or less than the remaining stops allow a player to move. You need to get an exact roll to land on home. The winner is the first player to complete the route and arrive at the Home station. This does mean you run the risk of spending a very long time at a station a couple of stops from your final destination. I suggest you take a good book with you. On arrival at the final point, the winner will then be in a position to have a celebratory beer while waiting to see just how long it takes the rest of the party to arrive. The more people that play this game the higher the likelihood that someone will bump you back to the start. Trial and error will determine the ideal number of players for any particular route. It would be very sad to play this game on your own.

Best Route – This game is a straightforward race between two or more players. Players agree their start station and end station, but then separately have to work out the best route to get between them. The first one to the destination is the winner. By way of example, you may have a start point of Wembley Park – in Zone 4 on both the Jubilee Line and the Metropolitan Line. The end point might be Goodge Street in Zone 1 on the Northern Line. Player 1 might go on the Metropolitan Line to Kings Cross. Then does he or she take the Piccadilly Line and change twice (Holborn for the Central Line then Tottenham Court Road for the Northern Line) or does he or she stay on the Piccadilly Line to Leicester Square and change straight onto the Northern Line? Meanwhile Player 2 might take the Jubilee Line to Bond Street (apparently shorter than the Metropolitan Line route, but with more stops) change to the Central Line to Tottenham Court Road then north on the Northern Line to Goodge Street. The possibilities are endless. Player 1, of course, may have double-crossed Player 2 and in fact got off the Metropolitan Line at Baker Street, having taken advantage of the fewer stops on this route and then switched to the Jubilee Line. Player 3 having dozed off, may have forgotten to get off the Jubilee Line and find himself in Stratford. This will almost certainly lose him the game, unless by some fluke the Central Line is out of action between Bond Street and Tottenham Court Road, allowing him to come sweeping back along the Central Line from the East and claim it was part of his strategy all along. This game has the added advantage of conveying a moral, covering both the nuances of Harry Beck's map and the vagaries of Tube operation – 'The best route is not necessarily the obvious one'. This is a useful first lesson for any commuter.

Tube Tag – In this game, you will need 1) An agreed route, including a number of agreed stops that must coincide with changes of Tube line 2) An appropriate travel card 3) Some time to kill.

Leaving from the agreed starting point, player one catches the first train and heads to the first agreed intersection. At this point, he leaves the train and makes his way to the platform of the connecting train to continue the journey. Player 2 leaves the starting point by the next available train and proceeds to 'follow' player one by Tube. If nothing delays his train, or he is able to make good time between Tube lines by going a different route to the platform, he may catch player one on the platform waiting for the next train. This is also likely if the Tube line you are transferring to has a more infrequent service. On catching player one, player two pronounces 'tag' and the game restarts from this point with Player two heading off first. This game is entirely pointless, but a good way to have fun on the Tube.

Mornington Crescent – What better game to play in its original setting? It would be foolhardy for me to go into all the rules here, as I can generally assume that the reader knows the important ones. You are not allowed to take the shortcut via Ealing Broadway when playing on the Tube and Rule 29 must always prevail over Rule 16. You should announce your arrival at Mornington Crescent loudly to the entire carriage, where as often as not, you will find others who wish to take part in the next round. Playing Mornington Crescent during stressful periods should be discouraged. This is a game that causes upset even between the best of friends. Invoking the Finnish variant of Hedgehog Road is not to be encouraged as the language barrier can cause confusion to the rules. It is also not advisable to try to engage other passengers in the verbal version of the game, as it is almost certain to lead to discord among passengers, particularly those who were not aware of special rule 23, which you have used to secure victory in three games in a row.

HISTORY OF THE TUBE

I am sure that I am not the only Tube traveller who has spent time wondering about the history of the Tube. Now I know that a recent addition was the Jubilee Line extension, because my journey changed as a result and not it should be said for the better. But whose idea was it? How did the idea come about? Who decided what to name each of the lines? Who chose the colour for each line? Who decided which places would get stations? Who decided that the map would be a work of distorted fiction? Who decided at what depth each line would run? Perhaps most importantly of all, who called it The Tube?

There are so many, for me, unanswered questions. I thought I would use this opportunity of shedding some light on these and other important matters for you. Have the laws of physics always been distorted below ground? Has it always been unacceptable to eat a ketchup laden bacon sandwich?

You may take what follows as fact, unless it is your specialist subject on 'Mastermind' or is a real life question on 'Who Wants to be a Millionaire?' In either of these instances, please trust that I know very little of any real value on this subject and if you rely on what follows and consequently lose on the £1m question, you have no grounds to sue me. For our mutual benefit when I started doing some research on the history of the Underground, I rapidly concluded that there are too many people, much better qualified than I am, to inform you on this subject. I also realised that there are a lot of people who take London Underground, as a subject, very seriously. I have probably already offended them, along with many others. I would just like to reassure enthusiasts at this point, that I do not intend my musings in any way to be disrespectful, or cause offence. I also realise that at this point, it is probably important to note that you should not take my representation of the history too seriously. There are many sources providing a fascinating, real, history of the Underground and I cannot recommend highly enough Transport for London's own website. I found myself getting quite engrossed as I started reading and my level of respect for those running this enterprise reached very high levels. However, I reluctantly reminded myself of the purpose of my mission. Here follows the Author's Official Misrepresentation of the History of the London Underground.

In the beginning was the commuter – And The Mayor said, "I will create the Underground in six days and on the seventh day I will rest." And darkness covered the Underground and due to a strange engineering fault on day two, it still does.

We were the very reason that they invented the Underground. Not for profit, not to be the first in the world, not because it would be fun, no, the Tube was invented as a better way to get you and me out and about on our travels around London, faster than we could before. Something to do with congestion. Who says history doesn't repeat itself? Particularly when you find the way they solved the congestion problem was to dig the roads up in the name of improving the transport system. Then they found that the more they improved the transport system, the worse the congestion became. There may be a lesson in here for all of us!

Then came some train companies with an idea – Unlike the Underground of today, there were a number of train companies and they all began to have ideas. First of all, one company came up with the idea of further worsening the congestion by blocking roads with construction traffic to build a line close to the surface. Then when they opened the line, they could take all the road works away and say, "Look how much we've improved congestion by." And who said there was nothing new in the world of politics? In many streets of London, just beneath the surface lie some lovely red brick tunnels. Here I learnt that the oldest section is from Paddington to Farringdon and was opened in January 1863. Why there? Why not in central London? Maybe it was simply easier due to available land; maybe the clerk of works lived near Paddington and needed to get to Farringdon on a daily basis. Maybe one of the investors had a mistress there and needed a quicker route to get to and from seeing her.

In reality, I have absolutely no idea, but you have to start somewhere. This is your challenge for your next train journey, particularly if it is from Paddington to Farringdon; make up a story of the best reason you can think as to why that was the particular route chosen. If you want to obtain more space in the carriage, try discussing your theories with fellow passengers and see how much they move away from you.

Then came some more train companies with the same idea - this time they hit on the idea that if they drilled their holes deeper they could avoid the congestion on the surface and make better use of available space. The deepest point below ground is 67.4metres. However, this is not the deepest below sea level. Why this deep? Had they calculated that this was the perfect depth to achieve maximum velocity? Was it because it wasn't worth putting escalators in unless they were going a reasonable distance? Were they trying to get to 100m and just got fed up with tunnelling? In truth, there is a convenient layer of clay below London that made for better construction, but why let the truth get in the way of a good story?

In those early days, there were some very important differences. The Central Line was an orangey colour, on the map, rather than red and another line was red. Some of the stations had different names and they based the map on topographical reality. This just goes to show, if you try travelling with an out of date map you vastly increase the chance of getting lost. Particularly if it is the black and white edition, on which all the lines look much the same, unless you are good at differentiating between different patterns of dots and dashes or different shades of grey. Failing this, you may be the cause of an increase to the numbers entering a station and not coming out the same day.

How deep is thy Tube? – Sat around in an office in their Victorian clothing, a group of well-respected gentlemen of the community were found to be having the following discussion. From their accents, you can presume that some were northern industrialists who had moved to London to earn their fortune.

"I say we go for 20 metres down," Fred said scratching his head over the plans.

"Oh, very la de da. Nothing like showing you're ahead of your time. Round these parts we'd say nearer 60 feet," George retorted. "And what if the other lot pick the same depth? Can't have our tunnel meeting theirs now can we? It would make it too easy for the passengers if it was all at the same level and besides the trains might crash."

"There you go again, always safety, safety, safety with you. What about cost? I say 20 metres and if we start from both ends we'll get the work done in half the time."

"There you go again, proper little Channel Tunnel. What if the ends don't meet up, Mister la de da?" George by this time was showing signs of agitation, almost fit for a commuter.

"Well," pondered Fred, "then we run two lines that go to different places and make it look like that was the intention. We can quietly connect them later and provide the added interest of disused stations on the bits we don't need, with a long unnecessary walk between platforms."

With that, the work began and London has never been the same again.

What colour shall we be? – Now if you thought the discussion on how deep to go had the potential to get fraught, what about deciding what colour they were going to use to represent each line. You can just imagine the scene, a little bit like a group of children about to play a board game.

"If I can't be blue, I'm not letting anyone on my trains."

"I wanted to be red, but he's already got red. If I can't

have red I'm going to have a colour that's almost red."

"Can we change colours later in the game? Wait until everyone is used to you being red then change it to my line?"

"When we change colour can we change the name of the lines too, to make it harder?"

"I want to be mauve. Why can't I be mauve?"

Oh, the deviousness of it all and all just to confuse the gullible commuter.

The great Harry Beck – In a moment of foresight, a gentleman by the name of Harry Beck, more used to constructing electrical diagrams, discovered the ultimate way to confuse me. In 1933, he re-drew the map of the London Underground, basing it no longer on topographical reality but creating a whole new art form. Apparently, when first published, the London Underground bosses sought feedback from travellers in case they found the map difficult to understand. Why have they stopped asking? Now we all resort to carrying a London A-Z to help make sense of it, or more normally use the Underground map on the back of the A-Z so that we don't lose it. This is all part of entering the Twilight or more accurately the 'Tubelight Zone'. You think that the distortion is just a diagram on paper, but it isn't. When you go below ground, the whole earth around you distorts to fit the shape of Harry Beck's map. This point can be proved by drilling down from above – or possibly, up from underneath, to prevent missing where the tunnel goes. Try for example travelling due north of Shepherd's Bush and then drill down - you just see if you don't find Maida Vale Tube station below.

The next station is Aldwych – Or rather it isn't. This is one of many Ghost Stations. These are not stations at which you can see phantoms, though there are probably some of those, but stations that have themselves become deceased. The Underground moved on and they didn't. Sometimes extensions to lines routed them a different way, leaving odd stations cut off. Sometimes they simply became surplus to requirements. This will come as no comfort if you've had to trudge further than you would have liked, at the end of a long day. As your tired feet weigh heavy, as you struggle to complete your journey, think about the fact that there may once have been a train line going all the way to where you really wanted to get off, which would have saved you the walk you are now doing.

Then there are platforms that we stop using. It never dawned on me when the Jubilee Line stopped going to Charing Cross that there were still platforms there that would no longer be needed. They aren't the only ones. There are other stations with spare platforms, some are used for other purposes, some just stand idle.

While we're on the subject of platforms, I've often wondered why so many of them are single sided – surely this is more costly to build. Was it just for the sake of the revenue from the adverts on the opposite wall? They could have placed hoardings in the middle of the platform, separating the two sides.

Do you think stations live in fear of being sidelined? It's the inanimate object equivalent of redundancy. One minute they're important, appearing on all the maps, the next minute one of their platforms isn't required anymore and before they know it, they're a ghost station. It's like they don't exist anymore, gone 'underground' so to speak.

Humour

Humour occurs throughout your Tube experience, if you know where to look. There are the times when your usual route is out of action from the starting point. Why in this situation does everyone wait until you have gone as far as paying for a ticket and getting to the gate before they tell you that no trains are running? Now correct me if I'm wrong, but this state of affairs is unlikely to have arisen between you buying a ticket and walking the ten yards to the barrier. Would it have spoilt the ticket seller's fun to have told you at the ticket office? If it weren't for the humour that can be obtained at the commuter's expense, the ticket machines could have been turned off, or at least have notices put on them explaining the situation.

There was the time they tipped us off the train due to an incident in Neasden. Why Neasden? Where is Neasden anyway? (This is of course a rhetorical question. From the fact that I was on the Jubilee Line, even I could work out that it was somewhere further along that line and must be somewhere near London, but it was not on my immediate route.) What worries me is the way people who regard London as 'home' take all these things in their stride. My fellow passengers seemed apparently indifferent as they calmly started leaving the Underground station in search of a bus. No thought appeared to be given to the poor people of Neasden in the grip of an 'incident'.

I unfortunately had no idea where I was, where to find a bus stop for buses heading in the right direction, let alone which numbered buses went in anything like my direction. This presents a bit of a problem in trying to catch the right bus. All of that would have been bad enough to deal with, quite apart from the other hundreds of people spilling out of the Underground Station with the same intent.

By my reckoning, I had two miles to walk. Even with the help of the A-Z, my chances were slim; I still needed to work out in which direction to walk.

On the survival front, regardless of whether you thought you knew where you were going, or who you were going with, this demonstrates the importance of carrying an A-Z and if possible a bus route map, together with a highly accurate compass. Alternatively, the phone number of a fast responding cab service may suffice. (However thinking about it, phone, fast response and cab are not words you would normally find in the same sentence.)

Underground humour also includes: 1) waiting until you're almost close enough to touch the train, having run down the escalator at break neck speed, then closing the doors just before you can get on. 2) announcing that due to signalling problems you should switch to another platform thirty seconds before the 'next train approaching' appears on the board, ensuring that the platform called is at least a forty second walk away.

I also wonder if Ticket Inspectors have a sixth sense. Why do they ask to see your ticket when you've lost it somewhere at the bottom of your bag? This is another of those scientific laws – don't ask me how it happens, but the law states 'That on any occasion that a ticket is requested to be shown, it will have condensed into a very small piece of paper at the farthest corner of your bag or pocket'. Now, I realise they cannot know that you've lost it at the bottom of your bag, but don't you think it's suspicious that they never ask to see it when you keep it in a handy pocket? I realise that as I need it for the exit barrier, I should always have it in a handy pocket, but I don't always have a handy pocket!

There is the possibility of humour at the expense of the passengers that would go far beyond any of the above occurrences. I have been expecting this to happen at any time. It may just be the way my mind works. This is a good reason why Transport for London should never recruit me to join the staff of London Underground, well not in a driving capacity anyway. Have you never thought of the possibilities? When you drive these trains there must be certain temptations. You could consider the following. 1) You could stop just past the station, or just before it, so that only certain passengers could get off. The mainline railways get away with it, with 'short platformed' stations, leaving you to drag your suitcase or bags along aisles that are too narrow, with the train lurching from side to side and you hitting every alternate person, on both sides, in the process, so why not do it on the Tube? 2) You could stop at the station and just not open the doors, so that passengers could see their stop but do nothing about it? You could always aggravate this with suitable commentary over the public address system. "This is Oxford Circus. You could get out here for shopping bargains on Oxford Street and Regent Street, but I've got to work so why should you be off enjoying yourselves." 3) This is the one I would not be able to resist. You could play announcements that didn't match where you were. "The next station is Kings Cross…." When in fact you are at Victoria, or "Change here for the Piccadilly Line…" when you're at a station that doesn't link to any other line. Just imagine the fun you could have and the chaos you could cause. My other favourite would be, "The next stop is Leicester Square, if you're going to see the movie at the Odeon, the ending is as follows… Have a pleasant evening." Alternatively, you could give announcements simply for the purpose of freaking out the passengers. Do you think the drivers ever want to give out Big Brother type comments on behalf of the carriages? "Excuse me miss, in the tight skirt and low cut blouse. This is the carriage speaking. Please cover yourself up, you're embarrassing me."

If I were the driver I would have a desperate urge to do something such as close the doors so the passengers couldn't get off and then say, "I'm new to this job, does anyone know the way to Victoria? And do I push the lever forward or back for reverse?"

IMPACT ON SANITY

If you don't have psychopathic tendencies before starting to use the Tube, you soon will have once you begin.

As I stand waiting for a Tube, which gives me a fair amount of time, I start watching the people around me and imagining what they do. It's a game anyone can play, although a vivid imagination is an advantage. A nervous disposition would be a positive disadvantage.

The dull looking chap on my left oozes an overwhelming sense of grey. He's clearly in banking. If he were just a couple of inches taller, he'd have done something interesting. The lady over there is definitely in advertising, sales at a guess. It's the 'I'll eat you for breakfast' look of confidence that gives that one away. The lady with more make-up than I own is definitely a 'Beauty' Consultant. There's nothing like advertising your own products. Then I find my mind wanders to the man at the edge of the platform, who is in the middle of a multi-million pound fraud that will be all over the papers in a few days' time. It's the way he's talking conspiratorially into his mobile phone and looking around in a furtive manner. Stood next to him, at a discreet distance, is an axe murderer. The chap next along must be a serial bigamist, given away by the rueful look and the packed lunch under each arm. I'd say this is just a normal day. More worrying is the prospect that others around me may be going through the same thought process, in which case I wonder what they have me down as. I just hope it's something more interesting than the truth, although the red hair usually helps on that count. They will at the very least have me down as having a wild uncontrollable temper. But what will they make of my survival rucksack? Will they have me down as a student or a foreign traveller? Perhaps if I start mumbling words to myself, out loud, in a foreign sounding dialect, it might help to get me more space in the carriage. The downside is they may give me no space at all in the carriage and I'll find myself standing here waiting for the next train in however many minutes time. At least if they do, there'll be another set of passengers to observe, maybe this lot will include a handsome prince who is desperate to make my acquaintance. I suppose it would be unreasonable to be disappointed that he hadn't brought his 'white charger' down onto the platform with him.

Whilst I realise that working on the Underground is very different from using it every day, I do wonder whether the employees look at passengers in the same light as I do. I hope for their sake that they at least start from the position of being mentally well-adjusted.

INSOMNIA AND TUBE TRAVEL

I have seen people apparently asleep on the Tube, but I have yet to learn their secret. I do suspect there is a large quantity of alcohol in there somewhere, or a medical condition causing them to fall asleep at inconvenient times and in awkward places. However, even without sleeping on the train itself, there are ways in which you can use Tube travel to your advantage and make it part of your survival strategy for life.

I stopped needing to count sheep at night whilst using the Tube. This was not, as you may think, because I was so worn out by my travels, or because I had found a lover in my carriage to take home at nights. The Tube gave me a way to deal with those long nights when you think sleep will never come. I developed a seriously worrying tendency. I started hearing voices in my head, disembodied voices, half human, half computer, announcing the stations. Had the Tube finally driven me mad? It is a possibility that I don't care to consider.

Even when I am on a Tube line that doesn't play the announcements, I can hear them. "The next station is Latimer Road." "The next station is Ladbroke Grove." "This is Westbourne Park." "Please mind the ga-ap between the train and the platform." Do you think it says ga-ap to give the feeling of the distance? And tell me, what kind of sick announcement tells you to mind the gap several seconds after the doors have opened and everyone has got off and potentially, fallen down it? "This is Royal Oak." "This is Paddington. Change at Paddington for mainline and suburban services" "This is Edgware Road. Change at Edgware Road for the District line." "Stand clear of the closing doors." "This is Baker Street change at Baker Street for..." I have even reached the point in my head of hearing the voice saying extra bits to the announcements, so it probably is a sign of madness. "This is Shepherd's Bush. Change at Shepherd's Bush for drug deals and mugging opportunities." I don't know about the mugging, but the brown envelope I witnessed being handed over made me wonder about the first bit. "This is Oxford Circus, please leave the train here for the opportunity of being ripped off by paying London prices for things you don't need." "This is Euston Station, please take all your belongings with you when leaving the train, unless you have items of real value that can in no way be mistaken for a bomb and which your fellow passengers will happily acquire." "This is Kings Cross, change here for the Hammersmith and City line and mainline rail services. Alight here for the Royal Institute for the Blind and just plain get off if you want to go anywhere else." "Please stand clear of the closing doors. And please ensure your rucksack is inside the doors when they close and not outside." I can even hear them now as I'm writing this. How did these help me going to sleep? Instead of counting sheep, I followed the continuous loop of the Circle Line and somewhere just past Tower Hill found that reality had blended into the world of dreams.

For those living in close proximity to the Tube and who are trying to sleep, it may not be so easy. You could of course limit your sleep to the hours that the Tube is closed. However, if you need to sleep outside these hours, might I suggest that if the noise and vibration are causing your insomnia, hearing station names or repeating announcements in your head may not be such a good idea. Counting stations may add to the aggravation. It may lead to an increase in your level of annoyance and drive you to add your name to the many who write to Transport for London to complain about the vibrations. I suppose it's possible that you may be one of the sleep deprived individuals I have seen asleep on the Tube itself. Perhaps if you're so used to the vibrations at home, you don't notice them on the train. Either way you have my sympathy.

JUDICIOUS IMPROVEMENTS TO THE TUBE

There is already a tremendous programme of improvement taking place on London's Underground and there is a danger that some of the foibles we know and love will be efficiently removed. However, at the same time there are always other areas that the authorities could focus their attention on, when looking for ways to improve the service. Here are a few suggestions to add to the debate:

1) Introduce a ban on boring adverts. All adverts should be interesting, useful, readable, amusing and preferably still valid. Of course, for the particularly amusing ones being out of date is much less of an issue.

2) The introduction of plants that can grow with no sunlight, but are still not made of plastic. Ones that resemble Triffids are probably best avoided. Perhaps some of the ones like Morning Glory, which flower on a daily basis for lengthy periods, could be encouraged to adapt to grow under artificial lights.

3) The inside of the tunnels could be turned into a planetarium with little dots of light for the stars. The

planetarium idea has the advantage of being more plausible than the previous suggestion of the street scene, as the inside of the Tube does feel like perpetual night-time.

4) Introduce an anthem for each station or line. This could be played instead of the usual announcements as the train approaches the station. This would have the added advantage that it would help improve the score of millions of people in 'Name that Tune' and similar games. Some would be obvious 'Underground overground Wombling free' for Wimbledon, although whether it should be for Wimbledon itself, Wimbledon Park or for that matter South Wimbledon might be a matter of huge debate. Gerry Rafferty singing 'Baker Street' would work well for Baker Street as would the theme tune from the seventies television programme 'Citizen Smith' when approaching Tooting. Some could be a little more ambiguous John Denver 'Leaving on a jet plane' for Heathrow, but then some passengers might think they were at London City Airport. Deliberate confusion could be added by playing songs like 'Ferry cross the Mersey' when crossing the Thames and a little closer to home 'London Bridge is falling down' when in fact the bridge itself has emigrated. Fans of Abba could be upset by the choice of 'Money' by Pink Floyd rather than 'Money, Money' at Bank, but then consoled by the use of 'Waterloo' at the eponymous station. Then of course, the lovers in the corner might like to listen to 'Up the Junction' by Squeeze before getting off at Clapham Common and for good measure a recording of some yodelling just before Swiss Cottage. For those stations that cannot find a suitable song or piece of music it would be a

good opportunity to invite local artists, or commuters with no musical talent, to enter a competition to develop one. This competition could then be televised and commuters could be voted off the carriage week by week until a passenger with a seat emerged as the winner.

5) Ticket machines could be 'voice activated' to save you fumbling around to work out which name the place you want is listed under. This gives the opportunity for confusion and with all the noise around, inevitably, mistakes could happen:

You speaking to the ticket machine, "I want a ticket to Westminster."

The Ticket machine then says in reply to you, "One ticket to Upminster."

You to machine, "No, I said Westminster please."

Then the Machine once again replies, "One ticket to Upminster via Plaistow."

Alternatively, you could get the unhelpful situation of it picking up the conversation of the people behind you, who have particularly loud voices and want a return ticket to Kew Gardens, rather than a single to Covent Garden. On a more positive note, the machine could be programmed with other messages such as, "I have eaten your money", or "I am really not working and there is no point in queuing here". This last one could be said loudly enough for the rest of the queue to hear, so that they can move away to queue in front of a broken, non-speaking, machine instead. When the machine is working and does successfully issue you the correct ticket it could tell you which direction on which line you should take to reach your destination and either how many stops it is, or where you should change. It could go as far as telling you how long you need to take to get to the platform in order to just miss the next train and how long you will have to wait for the next one. In fact, what is to stop it having a whole conversation with each person with the specific intention of winning the spot in the chart for the longest waiting times for tickets?

6) Transport for London could introduce film screens into the carriages and have a range of films showing on each train. At the front of the train it could be a 'U' rated film, progressing carriage by carriage through 'PG', '12', '12A', '15' and through to the rear carriage showing '18' rated movies for the lovers who wanted a bit of excitement. Alternatively, there could be one carriage showing horror movies where the brave hearted could almost certainly guarantee a seat, or failing that an extremely scary journey and the faint hearted would hide underneath the seats, thus getting more people into the carriage. Subjects involving things like murder on the subway might be considered most effective. There could also be showings of 'Speed', with runaway public transport and of course 'The Deep'. The biggest weakness of this proposal is that people would have to time their journeys very carefully to ensure they could get off without missing a crucial bit of the film and they would need to know what time train they needed to catch later to be able to carry on where they left off.

7) The other thought that comes to mind is to make the whole journey like an amusement park. The possibilities for this are endless. For some of the journey you could make it like one of the cinematic experiences in which you use projection to make it feel as though you are

somewhere entirely different. Your journey on the Northern line might be, on the smoother bits, a gentle flight in an aeroplane across meadows and valleys, dipping down across mountain streams and out over the ocean. As there are relatively few smooth runs of track on this line, this section of the trip might be relatively short. For the bumpier bits, it might become an old-fashioned wooden roller coaster, looping the loop and taking you upside down and then move swiftly into a downhill ski through forest paths, or skate boarding round obstacles. By the end of the journey, passengers would feel either exhilarated or totally weak-kneed, but whichever it was they would certainly have had their money's worth. The downside would be that school holidays would become a nightmare for ordinary passengers as thousands upon thousands of children travelled the Underground just for the fun of it.

8) The Tube could be extended to serve places not yet covered. Whilst realising at one time or another there have been proposals to cover a large number of places in London with the Tube, to the extent that there are whole books on that subject alone, there are places a little further away that might benefit from being brought in to the Tube network. You could run a line from Basildon in Essex into central London to meet up with the Central Line and call it the Basildon Bond Line. An extension out to Windsor would make it much easier for the Royal Family to get between their homes and one to Canvey Island would have Londoners rushing out to the country. On the other hand the route from Land's End to John O'Groats might prove an interesting one, with endless cyclists and walkers using it to get home. The biggest danger of

extending the network within London itself must be the question of 'at what point do all the tunnels meet up and the middle bit fall out?'

9) Vending machines could be introduced that serve hot, fresh bacon sandwiches. These would need servicing regularly to keep them in working order, as the promise of a hot bacon sandwich followed by the delivery of a napkin with a dollop of ketchup, but no sandwich, would be a big disappointment.

10) Transport for London already ties up with some suppliers to provide them with marketing opportunities that keep the traveller happy and make the Tube look good, with products such as free bottles of water in the summer. I think this concept could be taken much further with brands such as Kleenex, Beechams and Domestos to overcome the level of germs with which the traveller shares public transport, or perhaps Sure and Daz for a clean and odour free travelling public.

11) The free distribution of the newspaper Metro was subject to a tender process for the right to fill the afternoon slot, courtesy of the highest bid. Perhaps this should have been done on a station by station basis rather than the network as a whole. It would lead to a much better variety of reading material when you have forgotten to take anything better. In the absence of a process that goes into that much detail, preference should be given to publications with a much wider appeal such as The Beano.

12) The Underground could follow other railways and

introduce different classes of ticket. In the 'First Class' section, you could get a seat and enough room to open a broadsheet newspaper. In 'Standard class' you get a seat and enough room to read a small book. Finally in the 'Sub-standard class' section, you could get standing space and limited opportunity to breathe. Sub-standard would of course remain as currently priced, whilst Standard and First Classes could be appropriately priced to make up for the lost revenue from squeezing fewer people in.

KNOWLEDGE IS A WONDERFUL THING

If you have the opportunity to look on the internet before you set out, you can get advance warning that you're going to be delayed. The real-time information on the Transport for London website tells you which lines are delayed and the severity of the delay. You can choose the point at which to find another route, go and have dinner or settle down for the evening with a good book. Is a 'minor delay' in which you will have a 'noticeably longer journey time' or a 'severe delay' in which you can have a 'significantly longer journey time' or a 'Suspended' route in which you have no journey time at all, the point to make alternative plans? What happens if your journey involves a route that has good service followed by one with a 'severe delay'? Would this be the same as two journey legs that both involve a 'minor delay'? Then of course, what happens if you set off at the point it is a minor delay and while you're getting there, on a route with good service, the minor delay becomes a severe delay? If you had known this at the start, you might have been better starting by the route with the minor delay, as by the time you progressed along that route, the suspension would have cleared. There are so many difficult decisions to make as part of your daily travel.

One piece of information that the Transport for London site doesn't tell you is what the backlog of passengers is looking like. I don't mean whether they are tall, slender and good looking or small balding and fat. Perhaps the information on the website should be linked to the increased closed circuit television cameras being put into the stations. You could then have a look at the number of passengers jockeying for position on the platform, to decide whether you can face travelling at all. Of course, you would also be able to check if they were short, balding and fat, but that would not be the primary objective.

There is also an Internet page for the 'estimated time of arrival' of trains pulling into stations on particular lines. This is similar to the information that appears on the platform and I therefore assume it is subject to the same vagaries of Tube time. Helpfully on trying to look at it on one occasion, I was reassured to receive the message 'This feed is out of date', so I'm guessing it is similar to the platform information then!

It seems that by using the Internet, it is now possible to obtain information relevant to the underground systems in all different parts of the world. This may necessitate reading many and varied languages as, discomfortingly, with the exception of New York and more recently the London Underground, many sites do not cater for the non-indigenous population. New York may of course be catering for the variety of the indigenous population, if that is not a contradiction in terms. Where they do provide information in a non-native language, for the most part this, thankfully, is English and our ability to continue to be linguistically lazy is preserved. When reading the information the websites provide, some leave you convinced of their efficiency and it is for example easy to believe that the Tokyo system successfully transports nearly 9 million people a day. That is nearly three times the number of people carried in London. However, some underground information sites leave you with burning questions about other aspects of the city's life. In Los Angeles there is a 'Jury Pass System' that urges those on jury service to use the subway by saying 'Being a juror means taking tough decisions, such as choosing the best way to get to the courthouse.' You can see it now, on the one hand, from the evidence presented, is this person guilty of murder, or is there a possibility that he is completely innocent; on the other hand, shall I go home on the bus or the subway? Yes, I can see they might both be difficult choices. Whether I get home late is certainly 'beyond reasonable doubt' on many occasions.

Of all the sites available, Transport for London definitely gets my prize. It wins both on the information it provides, but for me far more importantly, they win for maintaining a sense a humour and an ability not to take themselves too seriously. I am however intrigued as to what made them choose the particular fifteen languages, other than English, in which the map is available. Why for example is it available in Greek but not in Dutch or Portuguese?

LOCATIONS

It's so easy to be taken in by Harry Beck's map. Fundamental to your successful travels will be to learn how wrong this would be. If you're tired and feel that the link between Bank and Monument is a useful short-cut to take on foot, don't be fooled. This is as much a contradiction as the distance placed between Bank and Mansion House on the Tube map. In the first case, you find yourself walking at least a ten-minute trek between the two 'adjoining' stations, a journey achieved more quickly and easily above ground. In the latter case, others, far worthier than I, have already pointed this out as an opportunity to trick an unsuspecting traveller. According to the dear Mr Beck's inspirational method of representing the London Underground, a journey which appears to be best achieved with a number of train stops and a couple of different Tube lines is also a ten minute walk if you do the journey above ground, in this case quicker than the below ground option. Then if you know an unsuspecting fan of the television programme Eastenders, try getting them to catch the Tube to the imaginary Walford East Station. See how long it takes them to work out that it's not real. "What do you mean not real? Of course Eastenders is real." I hear you cry. Yes of course it is. One day I will explain to you the truth about Eastenders, along with the truth about the Tooth Fairy and the truth about Father Christmas. However, whereas it was Mum or Dad behind both the tooth fairy and Father Christmas it would be very difficult for them to disguise themselves as 'Walford East', so maybe it is real after all.

Finding the platform for another Tube line within the same station can be just as confusing. If you go from the Hammersmith and City Line to the Bakerloo Line at Baker Street Station, this will involve going through corridors, down stairs, up stairs, along the platform for other Tube Lines, before eventually arriving at the right platform. It is easy to assume as you take this tortuous journey that you have gone the wrong way, but that does seem to be where the signs take you.

For the Brit travelling abroad and choosing to use the Tube / Underground / Metro / Subway / Rapid Transit System or whatever other name it has been given, the problems of station locations and indeed whole line locations can be complex. In New York, the Jamaica Line will not whisk you off to the Caribbean island of the same name and the Brighton Line will not bring you back to Blighty. It doesn't seem to matter what part of the world you are in the Underground defies logic.

Given that some stations seem to have platforms that are miles apart and only notionally in the same place, you have to wonder how it came about that, by contrast, there are on the same line two stations Leicester Square and Covent Garden that are just 260 metres apart. Is this recognition that even a hundred years ago theatre goers and those going out for a meal, either did not want to walk far, or were wearing shoes with heels that made walking impossible? If the latter applies to you, please take extra care when using the escalators that you don't get the heel caught in the mechanism, as this is one of the major causes of accidents on the Underground.

LONDON CONGESTION CHARGES

Once upon a time, you could drive into central London fearing only the traffic wardens and the taxi drivers. Oh, the good old days. Days before big red and white 'C's were painted on the road. For those of us who live outside London there wasn't a complex process that we could so unwittingly fall foul of, unless we drove a large vehicle with many seats, wholly unsuited to driving around a capital city alone.

In comparison to the Tube, the roads were never congested and even in rush hour, the roads were a positive joy. You could breathe in fumes, but at least they let you breathe. What benefit has been gained from the Congestion Charge? I haven't noticed more Tubes, or more carriages (a little impractical maybe, although if you can have ordinary trains that are longer than the station platforms why not the Tube?).

Maybe there should be a congestion charge to travel on the Tube at certain times of day. Maybe there should be special premium priced Tubes to allow breathing space at extra cost. As far as I can tell, the only winners from the congestion charge are the taxi drivers, although they don't seem to be overly thrilled by it either. You can now get to your destination reasonably quickly and without being squashed and jostled, as long as you can afford to get a cab. The workings of equality are wonderful to watch. The congestion charge is a transport policy for the rich. If you can afford it, you can travel more easily above ground by your own car or by taxi, meanwhile the rest of the world is crammed below ground out of sight.

So how do you survive in the face of the Congestion Charge? After much contemplation, the answer seems to be to obtain a sufficiently large vehicle to be exempt from the charge and stop using the Tube. On the downside, although movement will be easier and you can convert some of the seating into sleeping accommodation, you will need to keep moving, as nothing has been done to solve the problem of parking once within the congestion zone.

What no one seems to consider is the impact of providing public transport on congestion in the first place. As early as 1892, Thomas Curtis Clarke wrote "The better the service of street railways, the faster does the city population grow, the more do the people ride and the greater is the congestion of traffic and the louder the complaints of the public." Nothing new there then! By this formula, increasing the Congestion Charge to give more to spend on public transport will simply stimulate the vicious circle effect and in this instance 'circle' does not refer to the line of the same name that I have not yet experienced being vicious. (When I first wrote this due to a slight mistyping, the spellchecker changed the word vicious to viscous. In connection with the Tube, it might be interesting to consider the viscous Circle effect.)

Lost luggage

For the whole of London Transport, there are no fewer than 200,000 items of lost luggage dealt with in a year, which goes to show just how careless we all are. There is some luggage that you can understand leaving behind and there are other items that don't make nearly as much sense. I imagine mobile phones and keys slip out of pockets and are left regularly and for that matter books and reading glasses, but with other items, you sometimes have to wonder, for example, how do you leave a fourteen foot boat?

"Hello. This is the Left Luggage Department. How can we help you?"

"Oh, hello. I was just wondering if anyone had handed in a boat?"

"Are we talking a toy boat here, Sir?"

"No. It's about fourteen foot long. Hard to miss, except of course I must have missed it on the way off the Tube."

"Was that on the Victoria Line, Sir? I wouldn't want to go confusing it with any other fourteen foot boats."

"Yes, that's it. Can I come and collect it?"

"Yes sir. Can I just ask why you were carrying a fourteen foot boat on the Tube, Sir?"

"Well the weather forecast said it was going to rain

heavily and I couldn't fit an umbrella in my briefcase."

Quite apart from boats, wouldn't you think you might realise you hadn't got your glasses on, or that when you set off you were carrying a grandfather clock? On the other hand, I can understand what someone might have been doing carrying a park bench. They were ensuring that they would definitely get a seat, but you've got to wonder what the reaction of the person who left the wedding dress must have been when they realised they no longer had it. You can just see that being the end of a very happy relationship. You can hear it now.

"Darling, you know I said I spent £3,000 of our hard earned savings on my wedding dress. Well, I was not quite telling the truth, it was really £5,500. Oh and by the way, I left it on the Tube earlier and lost it. Do you think our wedding insurance will cover it?"

Having said that, the conversations where someone got home to find they had left cremation ashes on the Tube wouldn't be the easiest, particularly if they were being kind enough to transport them for someone else. Another living being that is, obviously it was someone else in the urn.

One statistic that doesn't bear thinking about is that in one year, there are almost 28,000 pieces of clothing left on public transport in London. How many of those do you think were London Underground boxer shorts?

Sadly, I can no longer find the section of the Transport for London website that gave information on luggage that had been left behind. It did make interesting reading, but has perhaps fallen victim to the need to discourage such absent-mindedness in the interests of security.

At his point, it is perhaps wise to introduce some

travel tips for luggage. Maybe the first piece of advice should be that in common with starting infant school, when travelling by Tube please ask your mum to sew those little name labels onto all your belongings and ensure that this is in conjunction with an up to date phone number or address. For larger or more valuable items, or maybe for those items that are most commonly lost, the next thing to do is have them micro chipped, or include some type of homing device that enables them to be identified, or better still located by you at a moment's notice. Gloves can be attached by a long piece of elastic to the ends of your coat sleeves, or running all the way through if you wish to wear the same gloves with different coats. The same trick could be used for a mobile phone on one end and a wallet on the other. I'm not sure what the best approach would be to stop you leaving a fourteen-foot boat, a stuffed eagle or a grandfather clock. Attaching this to your sleeve with a piece of elastic may lead to other incidents occurring.

The whole question of left luggage did make me wonder how many teddy bears are left and whether they're properly looked after until they're reunited with their distraught owners.

Maybe we'll get to the point one day where everyone's possessions are micro chipped, in order that they can be reunited with the minimum of fuss, with a small return fee being paid over. An owner could use a chip linked to a GPS system to locate their errant possessions. This would be a sort of bugging device for your teddy, or fourteen-foot boat as the case may be; although the GPS may not actually work until the item had already been brought back above ground.

Wouldn't it be nice to arrive home to a message on

the answer-phone, after a long day of losing your possessions, a nice voice saying, "Hello, it's the Left Luggage Department here. Just to reassure you that your grandfather clock and teddy bear have both been handed in. We have rewound the chimes and tucked teddy up in bed for the night, so if you would like to collect them in the morning we open again at 8.30. Have a nice day."

What happens to the items that don't get handed in? In some cases this is because another passenger has spotted an opportunity. However, do you think that the trains might have a life of their own, once we've all gone home? One in which somewhere they have sidings that are all brightly decorated, with dresses and other clothes for curtains, a bedside light, a rug and a few ornaments on a shelf? Places where the train makes use of our left luggage? When you start thinking like that, there are all sorts of possibilities. The little furry animals, that can be seen running around the rails, may be like 'The Borrowers' and have little homes using our dropped belongings for many imaginative purposes. I'm still not quite sure what they would do with a fourteen-foot boat.

Music

At least the Tube hasn't descended to the depths of playing piped music morning, noon and night. That would inevitably bring the psychopathic tendencies to a head much faster. The fact that it doesn't play this music means that I could even recommend it between the months of September and December as a place to escape the endless repetition of "So here it is, Merry Christmas". There is something very depressing about hearing Christmas music when you still have half a hope of a late summer heat wave. Although having now moved somewhere that doesn't seem to play any piped music at all, I have found I rather miss it.

I have experienced several types of music on the Tube, ranging from the bizarre to the plain intimidating. All of them loosely fall under the heading 'busking', but they offer such variety. There is the 'not altogether there' bloke, playing the tin whistle, one handed and therefore with only half the note range, most of which sound the same anyway. It makes 'name that tune' impossible however many bars of music you get. Then there's the guitar player, who by playing the more suicidal end of the love song range, takes away your sunny day, even without the confines of your underground travel arrangements.

I think a law should be passed allowing only buskers who play happy music and who can play all the notes of at least one complete piece. I have nothing against the bloke with one-hand, he could still play as long as he had his tin whistle adapted to his needs, or played songs within that note range. This would reduce the number of buskers, but would improve the travelling experience. Or would it?

London Underground does have a 'licensed busking scheme' where several hundred artists play at 39 designated sites. I'm guessing the other 463 sites are manned by the unlicensed buskers. As part of my 'charter for London', I propose a new busker test. I would only authorise to busk those who pass the test. The test, which would, of course, be set by me, could be varied as suited me, to ensure they couldn't just 'mug' up to pass the test and the decision of the judge is final. What do they say about power corrupting and absolute power corrupting absolutely? I would of course insist that buskers play only my favourite music and in the original format – no murdering of good music allowed. On the downside, this could cut, quite significantly, the number of buskers, licensed or otherwise, that are authorised to continue.

I presume thanks to the licensing scheme, occasionally, there is the sheer pleasure of real musicians, who you feel cheated by, in only getting to hear a few bars of music, as you are sucked into the bowels of the earth, down the escalator. It isn't so bad when they're at the bottom of the escalator, but when they're at the top, it feels as though they are the last vestiges of the living world being stolen from you as you descend into the underworld. Perhaps it would be wise to add earplugs to the rucksack, both to protect you from the not so good players and to save you being depressed as you desperately listen to the good ones fading away, as you are drawn into the chasm of the Tube. This is also the point of your journey that it would be in poor taste for them to play the Status Quo song 'Down, down, deeper and down'.

Underground busking seems to have become a career in its own right. I had always presumed that musicians use it to earn a little extra cash whilst they are studying, or whilst they are trying to get 'proper' concerts, but it seems that I am mistaken. For some, this is their proper concert and the way they make their living. Perhaps I should be giving it a little more attention, as a listener, not a player. If I started busking, you'd all start complaining. My childhood attempts at the violin were a travesty and it was only with my miniature bagpipes that I ever really summoned a tune.

Never stop to listen to the buskers, good or bad. It doesn't matter where you stand you will be in the way. People don't walk round you as much as through you and if you're there long enough, this soon becomes over you. It's amazing how people can develop similarities to bulldozers when they put their minds to it.

How do those famous artists that have filmed their pop videos on the Tube, or the big movies that have been filmed on undergrounds around the world, manage to do it? How do they manage not to get stuck in the stampede and instead end up with video footage of orderly commuters that haven't blocked the artists from camera? I am guessing in these instances the 'commuters' are all film extras, but how do they do it? They could of course film at night. From the lighting on the Underground, you have no idea what time of day it is. Perhaps they use some of the disused stations and platforms. Are any artists big enough to get London Underground to close a station or platform to the public purely for filming?

The most bizarre Tube music has to be on the train itself. Although this might refer to the 'Walkman' and 'I-pods' carried by my fellow travellers, which are played at volumes for the 'enjoyment' of all, sadly this is not the only music in the carriage; nor am I referring to the passengers who inadvertently whistle, entirely forgetting to be sullen. The type of music I am referring to, doesn't happen at rush hour, the players would never get in the carriage and if they did, getting their instruments out would be impossible. This type of music occurs in the afternoons and evenings. At these times, entire Romanian folk bands get on a carriage, play a number, pass round a hat and at the next stop switch to the next carriage. How do I know they are Romanian? Well I don't. For all I know they could have been born and bred in Hackney and dressed up as a Romanian folk group to fleece the gullible traveller. These are the ones I find intimidating. Somehow, the way the hat is thrust at you as they go round makes you feel as though something bad is going to happen if you don't give generously. However, when this is balanced against the something bad that can happen by getting your purse out on a Tube, I'll stick with the former fear, thank you.

Interestingly, once again the byelaws catch it all and state that 'Except with written permission from the Operator no person on the railway shall to the annoyance of any other person (i) sing or (ii) use any instrument, article or equipment for the production or reproduction of sound. With this in mind and taking what can be deemed as 'equipment' to an extreme, feel free to have the next passenger that audibly burps or farts in your general vicinity removed from the train, unless they have a written note permitting them to do so and for this purpose, they cannot have written the note for themselves. You may also deal with the person constantly tapping their foot or inadvertently singing along to their personal stereo in much the same way.

NAMING OF STATIONS

In the early days of the Tube, the stations were named after the locations at which they were based; sometimes this was a building such as the British Museum, sometimes it was a road name. Now please don't rush off thinking 'How convenient, I can get out at the British Museum', because you can't. It's one of the 'ghost stations'. What I can't work out is why they later changed some of the station names. No, this isn't the point to argue logically with me. I realise some places may have been knocked down and others built. I realise that it's not unknown for roads and areas to change their names according to their fortune, but that isn't my point. If you can get away with creating a map that bears no relation to the real location of the stations, why stop there? Why give stations names that bear any relation to where they are? When they moved the entrance to the Dover Street station round the corner, did they rename it "Round the Corner from Dover Street Station?" No, they called it Green Park. That could place it at any one of a number of points around the park or more logically right in the middle.

On the assumption that accuracy and precision are irrelevant, I have a proposal. Let's bring all station names up to date. There is no need to feel constrained by their location or any general reference to where they are. No, let's go the whole hog. Let's do to station names what Harry Beck did to the Tube map. Let's have names that bear no relation to reality. This is my charter for a new London, my manifesto for change. Let's re-name the stations along each line following a theme and with more interesting names than they have at present. Now in fairness this is partly inspired by some brilliant artwork at Tate Modern on this very subject, together with some other displays using maps of America and composite maps of the United Kingdom, but I digress. My plan is quite simple. Let's take, for example, the Piccadilly Line and change the station names to those of the England Rugby Team who won the Rugby World Cup in 2003. I realise time has moved on, but let's face it, we don't win things very often. It's either that or the 1966 Football World Cup. Arsenal might become 'Lawrence Dallaglio' Station (this would give me additional satisfaction being a rugby fan). Holloway Road might become 'Will Greenwood Station'; Caledonian Road would become 'Neil Back Station'. King's Cross / St Pancras being so central would become 'Jonny Wilkinson' Station and so on, with the obvious Leicester Square becoming the pride of Leicester 'Martin Johnson Station'. We could name the Hammersmith and City line after the 2008 Olympic medallists, with it now known as the Yachting, Cycling, Rowing and Swimming Line and then in 2040, when England has another global sporting triumph, we could rename the Jubilee Line. We will need a widespread sporting success before being able to replace all the names on the District Line; perhaps this could be the 2012 Olympics.

Now when you stop to think about this, the theory is all very well, but there are one or two complications. If each line has a theme, then any name for an intersecting station would need to be part of more than one theme. So following this thinking, Martin Johnson would also have to be part of the theme of the Northern Line, or at least that branch of it, which is the opposite branch to that of Jonny Wilkinson Station, but the lines then join up again at Euston before separating out again. Not so easy now, is it? I also seem to have put Jonny Wilkinson Station at the intersection of six different Underground Lines and two mainline stations, though fortunately the mainline railways at that point do at least take you north. On the upside of this practice, just think of the pleasure of being able to provide directions to a lost Australian backpacker and be able to say "Change to the 'Twenty Seventeen Line' at Jonny Wilkinson Station… Shall I just run through that again for you, to make sure you're clear?" This could further be enhanced by naming another line after the Ashes victories of 2005 and 2010 and so on. The fact that Australia has otherwise beaten us at everything would be quietly ignored, in true English fashion. We were great once.

Although it might take a long time to achieve, we could rename the Underground one line at a time when England has a major sporting victory. We could honour and immortalise our sporting heroes in a very 'down to earth' sort of way.

An alternative to this sporting theme would be to pick any subject matter for which the English are famous. Now of course this is subjective and you have to remember that I am proud to be English. We could have the Cheese Line, with Wensleydale, Double Gloucester, Red Leicester, Cheddar and of course Stilton. Then we could have the Great Political Leaders Line, with

Churchill, Disraeli, Gladstone, Lloyd George, Peel and so on. The fun is to try to work out the interconnecting stations, so for example is there a great political leader that is also a type of cheese, failing that could someone hurry up and invent a Disraeli Cheese. For good measure, Peel could be an intersection in the 'Fruit' Line. If you were able to concoct Disraeli Cheese that may qualify you to be part of the Inventors Line along with a mixture of old-timers such as William Web Ellis (rugby was an invention) and modern day greats like Dyson. To confuse the unsuspecting passenger you could have the Great Battlefields Line with stations such as Hastings, (it's the importance of the battle, not whether we won), Bosworth etc. There used to be a real irony that the station you came into if you got a train to England from France was Waterloo. For that reason if no other, it's almost a shame that the Eurostar has moved to St Pancras. I'm sure with a bit of imagination we could find all sorts of ways to offend our international travellers. We could, of course, rename St Pancras as Agincourt Station.

You can see it now, a lottery throughout the land, with the prize being to name the stations along an Underground line for 12 months and then next year they can all change to something else. This should be promoted by publishers of maps. Think what it could do for sales if everyone had to buy a new one each year. Wouldn't you just dread the year that a teenage punk rock fan won?

There is also the possibility of having the Premiership Line with stations being relegated or promoted on an annual basis. This would work well, until the real Arsenal underground station, had a change in fortune and became known as Wolverhampton Wanderers Station.

Some station names have been made famous by

certain television programmes and here I am not referring to Walford East. If the name of Tooting does not immediately bring to mind the opening scenes of 'Citizen Smith' you have never lived, or you're just too young, which is a less attractive thought.

Many countries give their underground lines numbers instead of names. Whilst this might in principle simplify things and may feel logical, this is contradicted by cities such as Beijing which at one point had lines 1, 2 and 13, but still planned to build 4, 5, 9 and 10. What do they have against the numbers 3, 6, 7, 8, 11 and 12?

OTHER PEOPLE ON THE TUBE

Now where I come from, talking to strangers is fine. My mum is always doing it. It gets embarrassing at times, but basically, it's ok – and what are parents for, if not to embarrass their children? Now in London, well it's different. In London, you do not talk to strangers and strangers who talk to you are either drunk, foreign, lonely, desperate or slightly crazy or some combination of them all. Thinking about it, in London you often don't talk to the people you know, let alone strangers.

London is a place of anonymity, don't talk, don't catch someone's eye, even body language is curbed in favour of a minimalist style of moving where necessity is the only reason to do anything. People walk around with their eyes downcast, or stare obliviously into space with a blank expression. They may stare up at the adverts or down at their shoes, but they never register the existence of a fellow passenger. Funny how close up you can be with someone on the Tube, how intimate (and at times I mean really intimate) and yet somehow the whole closeness is only all right if you don't look them in the eye and if you pretend to yourself they aren't real. It's a bit like going topless on a beach, it's fine as long as you don't know anyone there, but as soon as you strike up a conversation with someone and even get as far as exchanging names, topless is no longer a comfortable state of affairs. For reference, the anonymity does not make it acceptable to go topless on the Tube in any circumstances.

While London is a deeply impersonal place it is not as bad (if bad is the right expression) as I found Los Angeles. I was advised not to walk anywhere. To be fair that is partly because people just don't walk in LA and partly because of the fumes, but it is also because if you catch someone's eye you are likely to find they start following you. In comparison, London is actually a safe place to be friendly. You also find a whole range of people using the bus. The bus I caught in LA seemed to have just me as a normal passenger and some would dispute my normality. Then there were a number of 'down-and-outs' who seemed to be using the bus as a means of moving house, judging by the bin liners they were carrying with them. Perhaps on reflection that made them the ones that were normal and me the one that was odd.

Perhaps that's why lovers stand out so much. There is a flamboyance, a state of barefaced rebellion of showing intimacy, when surrounded by a city of cardboard cut-outs. They may be sweaty, smelly, jaded looking cardboard cut-outs by the end of the day, but cardboard none the less. My image of the city of London, as an exciting, vibrant place has been dashed by the realisation that anonymity is everything. It is hard to be both vibrant and anonymous at the same time.

There are few occasions that you see any real feeling amongst your fellow travellers. At the end of a long day, you may detect tension and then in the evening there may be some signs of excitement and laughter amongst those on the way to the theatre or for a night out on the town. The only time of the week you can witness more open feelings are on 'match days' when fans, sometimes from opposing teams are enclosed in a confined space on their way to or from seeing victory or defeat. Before a match, there is the noisy confidence of the 'win whatever the odds' mentality and afterwards there are the in-depth, sometimes drunken, discussions of the calibre of the referee, or the manager or the goalie or sometimes all three.

It can be quite fun trying to read the real body language of your fellow passengers. Once you get past their disgust at having to share their morning with you, what are they really thinking, what does that expression say? Is that mouth normally that shape or does it reserve that peculiar expression purely for commuting. Is it possible that the guy in the corner has a vacant expression on his face on a permanent basis? How many years did it take the gentleman behind the book to develop the perfect sneer? Search out the shape of the lines. Does that face normally smile? This was much easier to do before the days of Botox – now just searching for the lines can be a game in itself. You can of course play 'spot the face changed through plastic surgery'. You will probably be sharing a carriage with many a facelift and tummy tuck. If you can't spot any, don't despair, change the rules of the game to look for people who would benefit from a little nip or tuck and decide which bits of them you would change. Failing that, spend your time practising pulling the same facial expressions worn by your fellow passengers. This can not only be great fun and pass the time of the journey, but it can, if noticed, either secure you additional space in the carriage or, on a bad day, a punch on the nose.

Another approach to liven the day is to freak out

your fellow passengers by brightly and loudly saying, "Good Morning," as you crush your way into a carriage, or "Good Evening" at the end of the day. I can assure you that your fellow travellers will not be expecting it and you are more likely to receive blank stares than a response. What can be uncanny, is however loudly you may have spoken, your fellow travellers will respond as though they heard nothing.

Pets and the Tube

There is good news if you're a pet owner. You can take your pet on the Tube as long as you, or the pet, do not contravene the relevant byelaws. Of course, if you are not a pet owner, or pet lover, this may simply mean a greater degree of overcrowding and a sensation of arriving at work after a trip to London Zoo. For the owner of the pet, the first problem to overcome is 'does your animal need a ticket'? If you don't already know the answer, you're in good company. I don't know either. The regulations state that, "No person shall bring an animal on to the railway without a valid ticket for that animal, if the operator requires him to have a valid ticket for the carriage of such an animal." So that's clear then. Delightfully the byelaws go on to say that "Except with permission from the Operator or an authorised person, no person shall bring an animal on to the railway which, in the opinion of an authorised person may threaten, annoy, soil or damage any person or property." It seems that as long as your giraffe is not a part time thug you should be just fine.

Unfortunately, there is a requirement to carry your animal when on a moving escalator. Therefore, we can conclude that if your giraffe is full-grown, only take it when the escalator is broken or otherwise out of service.

I'm tempted to see what sort of animals you can get

away with. For a start, there is nothing to say who is an authorised person. Could I claim to be an authorised person and therefore authorise a small lion, for example, or a large one on days the escalators are out of action, or if the accompanying person is very strong? Alternatively, it could be fun to put to the test the removal of the offending animal by the 'authorised person' if you refuse to remove it yourself. You can just imagine the conversation. "Are you really planning to tell my lion he can't travel on this train, because he can get very ugly when he's angry and I have no wish to tell him?"

An alternative view of all this is that the same rules should apply to children and drunken revellers. Basically, if there is a risk that they might annoy someone or soil or damage property they should not be allowed to travel, that would really cut down the congestion.

When I think about it, most morning commuters annoy me. Can I have them removed so that I can have the carriage to myself please?

The other thought that springs to mind is the chaos that could ensue even amongst legitimate pets. All it would take would be a couple of pet mice or rats, suitably caged, a couple of cats on the way to the vet and a few dogs on the way to a dog show and what were otherwise civilised pets become a mad chaotic party. The noise would be considerable and the general agitation as the dog tried to get the cat, which was trying to get the mouse, could be utter bedlam. Then what would happen if a stray ferret was also thrown into the equation and was at that point in search of a pair of trousers to hide down. I wonder how the giraffe would be reacting to it all, although he may be too nervous about the lion to notice.

It also makes you wonder how many animals are left

on the Tube in a year and whether the rats and mice are ever reunited with their owners, or whether they take the opportunity to go native, so to speak and rush to join the other rats that live around the train tracks.

It is reputed that there are pigeons that make unaccompanied journeys by Tube for a couple of stations to reach better feeding areas. This would take the concept of homing pigeons into completely new areas. It would also seem that making it illegal to feed the pigeons in certain parts of London would be pointless, as they would just catch the Tube to find some food in a neighbouring area and then catch the Tube back to their preferred sleeping quarters later. The only solution to this would be to implement stiff penalties for pigeons found who were not in possession of the proper ticket to go hand in hand, (or hand in claw as appropriate) with the feeding restrictions.

There is another approach to adopt if you are trying to secure more space. Part way through your journey, remove a matchbox from your pocket, turn to a more nervous looking passenger and say, "Would you like to see my pet spider?" As soon as the train stops, at least a few additional people will leave the carriage than had originally intended to. If you made it a larger box and a tarantula, you could probably get the carriage to yourself.

Philosophy

Just a few random thoughts that go through my mind while I'm commuting and have nothing better to do than allow random thoughts to go through my mind. This may be the point that you become concerned that commuting has seriously affected my sanity, as no such thoughts go through your mind. If this is the case, don't worry, it will happen in time and in the meantime I'm glad you can share in mine.

- Is boredom a bad thing or the body's natural mechanism to stop you wasting time?
- Why can you always answer the £1m question when you aren't on the show?
- Why do the lights on Tube trains flicker on and off all the time?
- What road was the chicken crossing anyway?
- How many people do you meet in a lifetime? (Particularly relevant if you spend your days pushed up against complete strangers on the Tube.)
- If someone who likes cars is called 'a petrol-head' why isn't someone who likes flowers called 'a pollen-head', or someone who likes cooking 'a cooker-head', or should that be 'cooker-hood'?

- Who are the lovers in the corner of the carriage?
- If we measure area in square feet or square meters, why don't we measure the density of population in square people?
- Why is the hotel room that is allocated to you, always the one that is right at the end of the corridor, even when the hotel is apparently empty?
- Is there a subway in Oslo where in the summer months hundreds of Brits are to be found in pin stripe suits and bowler hats carrying the requisite briefcase and brolly?
- If 150,000 people per hour enter the Tube, how many come out?

PLATFORM POSITIONING

There is a science to correct positioning on the platform when awaiting an incoming train. In a study, it has been revealed that there are a number of points to take into account when determining the optimum waiting position. The study, of course, was undertaken by me, which just proves the point of what happens when a person has too much time on her hands

1) Select a position that no one is standing in yet. Pushing people out of the way, or standing on top of them is not well regarded. Alternatively, smelling the way my dog does, when he needs a bath, may mean that if you stand on a crowded spot, everyone around you will move.

2) Most people do not move away from the point on the platform that they first reach. They enter the platform through an arch and from that spot clamber on to the carriage that stops in front of them. If you know where, along the length of the train, these points fall at all preceding stations, you can derive from this the carriages that are most likely to be full. You can then move to stand at an appropriate point to find a more empty carriage to get into. This may require considerable research and additional time spent on Tube trains. Alternatively, it is a good use of time spent on the return journey, when due to falling asleep on the train, you have overshot your normal

stop. This either means you have developed the knack of sleeping standing up or that it is one of the rare occasions you get a seat, only to spoil the perfect journey by waking up to find you are in Epping when you should have got off at Mile End.

3) The quietest point on the platform will leave you the fewest number of people to fight off in order to get on the train. That is unless you have picked the point that is furthest from any opening door and you still have to make your way to the back of the crowd before starting to fight them off.

4) Finally, my favourite trick is to pick the correct point on the platform, which is parallel with the doors of the train that align with the exit point of the station at which I will depart the train. (You may need to read this sentence several times, but it does make sense – to me anyway.) This ensures that if all else fails, you will not be caught in the crush the other end, when getting away from the platform. You will have a head start on your fellow passengers, even without going up the "No Exit" way out. To follow this approach you will start to understand just how important the adverts on the platform are. The position of the adverts allows you to coordinate exactly where to stand. It's so much easier than counting the number of bricks along from a certain pillar or arch. When they took down the poster for Celine Dion and replaced her with one for a holiday in Sicily, it wreaked havoc with my positioning for several days. Standing next to the 'C' in the third poster along just hadn't been enough detail to memorise. If I'd remembered it was the C of Celine, I would have realised a lot sooner that they had changed the poster, rather than in my half-wakeful state assuming that they had moved the exit.

Lovers Take up Less Space

Even in this state, moving the exit had seemed a very strange thing to do, although not entirely improbable.

QUEENS, KINGS AND 'A' LIST CELEBRITIES

If mornings find my imagination running away faster than a plot in a bad crime novel, seeing myself surrounded by axe murderers and fraudsters, what happens on the journey home? Thanks to a day staring at a computer screen, by now my eyes are tired and ready for action, or inaction, as the case may be. I find myself looking round, once again, at my fellow travellers.

Suddenly, as if by magic, I recognise every other Tube passenger in my carriage. Tonight, for example in the corner is Michael Caine, deep in conversation with a guy I used to work with and one of my cousins who now lives in Australia. The couple in the corner seem familiar. I wasn't aware that that particular celebrity couple would ever consider using the Tube and what a coincidence that they're in London at the moment. Further along David Beckham is reading the Financial Times and Her Majesty the Queen has at least managed to get a seat. A friend's brother is just opposite, sitting next to Daley Thompson. Strange thing is none of them seems to recognise me. Of course, if they did, being London, they wouldn't show it. If any of the celebrities had recognised me it would have come as more of a shock to me than it would to you. It is fair to say I don't know any of them, but then in the

Underground 'other world' maybe I do. Maybe it's only above ground that they wouldn't have the least idea who I am. The other strange thing is that, by tomorrow, once I have had chance to rest my eyes and be more in the mood to join them for a chat, I will find myself back in a carriage full of strangers. It's the same pattern every day. Is the answer to make myself more sociable on the journeys home? You can imagine the reaction now if I were to go up and introduce myself to the ones that look like celebrities. Would they take it as a compliment that in my worn out state they look like someone famous or would it just make them edge that little bit further away?

There must be times that real famous people use the Tube. Do you think there is a culture amongst train drivers in the same way there is with taxi drivers of, "You'll never guess who I had in the third carriage of my train the other day?" Perhaps they should tell the whole train over the announcement system in the same way that cabbies feel the need to tell every subsequent passenger. I suppose it gives them a better story to 'dine out' on than saying, "You wouldn't believe how many rats I saw in the tunnels yesterday."

I wonder if there have ever been times when members of the Royal Family have disguised themselves and gone out to see what the Tube is like in rush hour. It's a shocking thought that it might have been Her Majesty's toe, that I trod on last week.

Rage

Way back at the start of my training in commuting by Tube, there was still a lot I had to learn. There were no guide-books that could have prepared me for some of the Underground experiences I was going to encounter. Even a book that included a comprehensive 'scratch and sniff' section would fall a long way short of reality.

There I was, having secured a small space in a carriage, when I turned and realised how essential it was to choose my direction of travel carefully. There were new experiences I needed to avoid. I found myself with my face pressed into the armpit of some big hairy bloke. I can tell you that this is not my favourite position for travelling, but on that occasion, it was all that was available and I was in no position to argue.

My research suggests that mornings aren't quite so bad as evenings. Most people at least wash and some even change their shirts, before going to work. There are those that you suspect are going to work in the same shirt they slept in and wherever it was they spent the night, they may not have had a bar of soap with them. These are the people to avoid at all cost. This is another situation when the outside temperature is an important factor in how unbearable your journey will be. Perhaps an additional 'byelaw' could be squeezed into London Underground's regulations, for all passengers choosing to travel by Tube. It would state 'All passengers commit to showering at least once in any 24 hour period in which they may wish to use the Tube'. I would prefer it to read 'All passengers commit to showering and changing into a full set of clean clothes before every journey. They also commit to using an effective antiperspirant and deodorant,' but I may be becoming a little unreasonable now.

Once I looked away from the suffocating armpit, I found myself looking down on a gentleman, who in turn looked down on a tiny, oriental lady pressed into the other corner of the door. This lady, minute as she was, was reading a book held no more than four inches (about ten centimetres for younger and foreign readers) from her face. The carriage was packed and uncomfortable and psychopathic tendencies had long since started to fester just below the surface, as I witnessed my first instance of Tube rage.

'Live and let live' is not the rush–hour motto of the Tube. The 'gentle' man, showing nothing gentle in his person at all, accused the woman of taking up too much space by trying to read. The fact that her person took up so little space didn't seem to come into the equation. It would all have been so much easier and rather more friendly, if he had just invited her to become his lover and dispense with the book.

Things started to turn nasty and I was left with an important decision. Should I intervene and stand up for this poor, exploited lady? She had done nothing wrong and she was in need of moral support. Should I perhaps force my way to stand between the man and woman to shield her from his wrath? Alternatively, should I do the honourable thing? I chose the latter, avoided the conflict and got off at the next stop to create more space. In situations such as these, all the best survival manuals will tell you, there is nothing wrong with being a coward and I had plenty of time to dwell on that thought as I waited for the next train.

Why do men think they have the right to pinch a girl's bum when in a confined space? It may be true that a woman will think about pinching a bloke's bum, but generally, she doesn't do it. Does the age of equality mean that it should no longer be all right for a bloke to pinch a girl's bum, or does it mean that it is now acceptable for it to work the other way round as well? Either way, it is amazing Tube rage is not more prevalent than appears to be the case.

I think that 'Tube rage' should be reserved for those passengers travelling with bacon sandwiches, coated in ketchup, who are not prepared to share them with other passengers. It doesn't matter whether you thought you were hungry before being accosted by the smell of a bacon sandwich, you definitely are afterwards. This type of Tube rage would be justified. Most people, even some vegetarians, are aware of the impact on the taste buds of the smell of warm bacon, drifting into the nostrils. It is torture to inflict this on your fellow passengers without offering to let them have a nibble of the corner. I'm not even going to begin to consider what an acceptable response is if they proceed to drip ketchup onto you, having not offered you any of the delicious, aforementioned, bacon sandwich. For reference, dripping ketchup onto someone is never acceptable, even if you have offered the sandwich to the passenger concerned.

I suppose Tube rage is much like any other syndrome. People with just causes to be angry make the least noise and those who shout loudest are the ones who have least to complain about. I have never heard a disabled passenger shouting about the inadequacy of their facilities, or a blind passenger shouting because they can't read the signs or for that matter even get near them to feel if there is any Braille, due to the throngs of people steamrollering everyone in their path. Using the Underground is not for the faint hearted.

The Underground staff should weed out people who are in a bad mood at the turnstile and never let them get near a train. It would not be difficult to do. If you made all the turnstiles 'faulty', rather than just some of them, you would soon get to find who was placid enough to travel. Anyone failing the test should be sent to get a taxi, on his own and at his own cost. My apologies to all the taxi drivers out there, but at least you can turn the intercom off and leave them in their own little world in the back of the cab, to rant noiselessly to themselves.

An alternative approach might be for Transport for London to train thousands of staff in 'anger management' techniques and have them on hand in every carriage, to provide counselling and support to stressed commuters.

Reading

Failing to carry your own reading material on the Tube will leave you at the mercy of the small selection of adverts around the carriage, or indebted to any of your fellow passengers that hold their own reading material at such an angle as to make it possible for you to read along with them. In reality, it is obligatory to have something with you to read on the Tube. The smaller the item, the better it will be received by your fellow passengers. For example, a book is good and a broadsheet newspaper is bad, particularly in rush hour. It's all about the amount of additional space it takes up. If you have forgotten to take any of the normal items, rummaging through your bag, or pockets, for old till receipts and shopping lists will suffice.

Your reading material will be better received if the print is large enough to be read from a distance by the person who forgot to take something with them and if it is an item of general interest. This normally rules out till receipts, but probably not cash point receipts. Interesting pictures are also appreciated, although what will be considered interesting will depend on the audience. You should also ensure, before turning the page, that you look around to be certain that everyone is ready to move on. Do not expect any acknowledgement from your fellow passengers, as they will pretend they were not reading your book or paper and will turn away until you have turned the page and are continuing reading. It was so frustrating to read the line "I'm sorry Kate, I can't give you what you want" and to end up having to leave the train without ever finding out what it was that Kate wanted.

Speed-reading is not an acceptable practice to fellow passengers, nor is anything by Jeffrey Archer or Maeve Binchy. Jackie Collins and Joanna Trollope are read at your own risk. Group participation in such matters is as inadvisable as is reading the article in Cosmopolitan on "The best sex you've ever had", unless this is the way you can cope with the antics of the lovers in the corner of the carriage. Show the article to the lovers in the corner at your own risk.

One thing I have noticed is that the quality of the reading material has gone downhill since the introduction of the 'Metro' as a free paper. For passengers without their own reading matter, on a long journey there is now less variety to read over other people's shoulders. Once you've read one copy of the Metro you don't need to read it again for several days. The introduction of other free newspapers at least gave the pretence of alternatives, but in reality there isn't much to choose between them.

One final suggestion, this book is not considered good reading material whilst travelling on the Tube. Most people survive the Tube by stopping noticing the things around them, developing an immunity to it and a thick outer shell. Reading this book could cause the grave risk of starting to notice all those annoying little habits and as I've already warned, leading to the development of strange psychopathic tendencies. On the other hand, in the hope that you're amused by it, spontaneous laughter ranks closely with talking out loud to yourself and singing, as methods of securing additional space as fellow passengers move away.

For the pessimistic amongst you who expect extensive delays, although War and Peace may be the obvious choice, unless you are reading it in the electronic form, just remember you have to carry it, together with the oxygen tank, food, maps, clothes etc.

London Underground does provide you with Poems on the Underground to keep you occupied at least briefly, however these are far too few to occupy the whole journey. The lovers or potential lovers would have enjoyed the two months with poems that "...explore the cause and effect of human passion". On second thoughts, the lovers may have been too busy undertaking their own exploration to notice any reading material.

Writing on the Tube is also best avoided, unless solely for your own benefit. The likelihood is that your writing will resemble that of a small child. If writing anything that will be read by others, it is best to do this on a device with a small keyboard in order that it is in fact readable. This will prevent the recipient being impressed that a 'five year old' could demonstrate such insight/ complete the form/ write up notes of a meeting/ or write on your behalf to your aunt in New Zealand.

It is also advisable to write about non-confidential matters, as your writing will provide reading material for the person who has forgotten to take a book of their own. It is always interesting to take the opportunity to read your neighbour's diary. This is how I discovered that the bloke next to me was going to Bristol at the weekend for 'Ian's dad's birthday', but wasn't doing anything interesting today, unless of course he was a pickpocket who was reading somebody else's diary. If you do have to read or write things that you would rather keep confidential, learn to write in code or in some remote language that hasn't yet reached London. This last strategy is unlikely, as the wonderful cultural mix that is London, means almost every language is spoken somewhere. Devising a secret code is more effective, but may get you hauled up and questioned about spying activities. Trying to convince the police or secret services that the document in code is only your shopping list may prove difficult. Whilst you may be able to supply them with the key that demonstrates that it says "Cornflakes, bread, lemonade, steak, bacon, ketchup...," You then have to convince them that each item represents what it says and doesn't have some complex double meaning. Why, after all, would anyone write his or her shopping list using a secret code?

SAFETY ANNOUNCEMENTS

When you travel by plane, you always start with important safety announcements before setting off. This has always struck me as strange, as, for a start, air travel is supposed to be one of the safest methods of travel and secondly if your plane is about to crash, how much difference does it make to adopt the brace position? Despite this, aircraft announcements are taken very seriously. If you use the Channel Tunnel there is a similar routine in telling you what to do if you hear the alarm. Why then on other forms of public transport are the same precautions not taken?

You get on a bus, train, ferry or Tube and no one says a word about safety, except at best to tell you to read some notices somewhere on the wall. Would it not be more use to provide instructions on these types of transport, where following the guidelines might make some difference to your chances of survival or at best injury prevention? On the Tube, having stewards or stewardesses in every carriage trying to demonstrate the exits, by waving their arms in the air, may prove difficult, particularly in rush hour and it wouldn't be the most enjoyable job for a man or woman to do. You also have the added problem of having to repeat the announcement after every station and of course in every carriage, but there is no reason that a brief safety message could not be given over the speakers. In order to increase the frustration for foreign passengers the announcements should be given out in English and use as many unusual English words and colloquialisms as possible. The language should be absolutely English English, in order to confuse the American travellers as well.

After serious thought, I think the following announcement should be made at regular intervals throughout the journey:

"Ladies and gentlemen, please listen carefully to the following safety announcement brought to you courtesy of Your Favourite Health or Travel Insurance. Please sit on the seats provided, or use the straps above your head for support while travelling. You will have observed that there are no seatbelts. This does not normally cause a problem. Short people should be given preference for the seats as we have made it impossible for them to reach the straps. The maximum number of people in any one carriage should be xx. If you were the last person to join a carriage that now has more than this number, please leave the train immediately and patiently wait in an orderly fashion for the next train. Alternatively, if you can be quick enough, please leave this carriage and rejoin the train in a carriage with fewer people and before the announcement to tell you to 'stand clear of the closing doors'. This carriage is designed to carry no more than (xx minus twenty) passengers. Any in excess of that number travel at their own risk. Please stand clear of the closing doors and ensure all rucksacks have joined you inside the carriage. In the event of a power failure, you will be plunged into complete darkness in the stationary position. Please do not panic. These situations are normal underground procedure and rarely last more than ten minutes. Should this situation continue, it is permissible for passengers to drop their blank expressions and start to communicate nervously with fellow passengers. In this event, once the service is resumed, it is considered good practice to re-adopt the blank expressions and pretend that no words have been exchanged with strangers. In such situations, it remains inappropriate to grope a fellow passenger even if they cannot see who is doing it.

Please place all luggage in a position where it is least likely to cause obstruction. Any claims brought as a result of passengers tripping over luggage will be the responsibility of the person carrying the luggage. The same applies to passengers injured by people wearing rucksacks turning round and knocking out their fellow passengers. Oxygen masks are not provided and in the event of flood, there are no lifejackets under your seats. In the event of a complete failure of the Tube you will be guided to safety by the conscientious employees of this Tube service who will explain to you which is the 'Live rail' and therefore not to be stepped on. Failure to take notice of this instruction will be entirely at the passenger's own risk. A combination of a flood and the live rail is not covered within this announcement, please refer to the main safety handbook in the unlikely event that such a situation arises. This handbook is available for sale at all good newsstands for the reasonable price of £63.82. Please enjoy your journey and thank you for letting the Underground take you for a ride. For the benefit of our overseas passengers g'day, au revoir and have a nice day."

Whilst we are on the subject of safety announcements, I know this may not be a good time to

Lovers Take up Less Space

raise it, but am I the only person who is astounded that there are no Government safety restrictions on the numbers of passengers allowed to travel in the carriage of a Tube train? Every bus has the maximum numbers for seated and standing passengers displayed. Why are Tube carriages treated differently? Of course if you are reading this whilst squashed up against the doors of a departing Tube, that is a thought you may have wished I hadn't had, or at least hadn't written down.

You will find on the Transport for London website 'Rolling Stock Data Sheets' that tell you about all the different trains in operation and provide useful information on the 'maximum observed standing capacity' the 'maximum full load standing capacity' and the 'theoretical crush standing capacity'. You may be interested to know that these are respectively 5, 6 or 7 people per square metre. Frankly, I feel overcrowded with anything much more than two people per square metre. As an additional game for the next time you travel in rush hour, take a tape measure, measure out a square metre of carriage and see how many people you can fit into the space. The website does not state whether you should make allowance for any luggage.

SCIENCE AND THE TUBE

Another interesting facet of the Tube is that no normal laws of science apply. With apologies to those of you who genuinely understand these things, there seems to be none of your "Matter is neither created nor destroyed in the course of chemical action", E equalling MC2, or any rule governing space, time, weather patterns, or distance, in operation on the Underground.

In my experience, a great deal of matter seems to be both created and destroyed during the use of the Tube. Dirt, germs and unpleasant odours seem to create themselves, whilst my sanity is the first thing to be destroyed. Matter is not just 'created', it's left everywhere that you don't want to find it and if you've ever held onto the wrong bit of seat and encountered the feeling of chewing gum sticking to your fingers, you'll know what I mean.

When it comes to going Underground there's none of your 'Wombling free' where the Tube is concerned. Uncle Bulgaria would have been distressed by how far from 'free' he would have felt, with the lack of space, paying for his ticket and the sheer heat of his furry coat, if, that is, he'd ever found the time to stop picking up the litter.

When it comes to the laws of science and the Tube, all bets are off and the only rule to follow is, 'There are no rules', except of course for the many 'byelaws' governing the Tube which should be followed without fail.

SIGNS

In this section, I am referring to the signs inside Tube Stations, rather than the ones showing you where to find the station. Tube signs are very important, even if misleading or difficult to understand. They start from the assumption that you have half an idea of what you're doing. On the platform, they may for example point to the 'Exit' or to other platforms for other tube lines. So far so good. However sometimes this is 'Exit to X Road and Y Tube line' in one direction and 'Exit to A Street and B Tube line' in the opposite direction. How many times of selecting the wrong exit is it going to be before I memorise the page of the A-Z, so that I know what street I am supposed to come out on? I just know I need to get out at that Tube stop. What more do Transport for London expect of me? Don't they realise that they are setting those expectations too high and I am not as competent as they think?

When you do find the right exit from the platform and work your way to ground level, you may be faced with other geographical questions. Do you want A Street (east) or A Street (west)? Do Transport for London have no idea how disorientating being underground can be? I barely know my left from my right when I come out, let alone east from west. Is this perhaps why some mobile phones now come fitted with a compass? You would think that if you picked the wrong one, it wouldn't be too difficult to cross the road, after all, cars stop at Zebra crossings don't they? Oh! How naive am I? You could try carrying a roll up black and white striped rug together with one of your very own crossing 'lollipops' and march out into the traffic holding it aloft. The lollipop not the rug. The danger with this would be that groups of small children might gather around you at the side of the road waiting for you to escort them across. For safety, add to your survival rucksack a compass, or a rope that you can craft into a bridge to sling between two buildings in order to cross the road. I know it would be much easier to go back down into the bowels of the earth and return to the surface by the correct entrance, but this results in loss of face and you have to admit to the world that you have no idea where you are. Whereas with the rope bridge you can significantly improve your image, as passers-by stand in awe and amazement as you scale one building, then throw the bridge you've just made, across the street, neatly catching it on the railing of the building opposite. Then they watch aghast, as you cross the bridge before rolling it up and putting it back in your rucksack, to the sound of spontaneous applause. On the other hand I may have been watching too many cartoon adventures.

Back in reality, there is the sheer arrogance of it all. It will not take many trips by Tube to realise that many of the passengers are foreign visitors to the city of London. Do we help them? Do we make concessions? Do we try to make their lives easier? Absolutely not. We wouldn't be English if we did. Every sign is in English. Many signs around this country in airports, stations and the Underground are not even in proper English to make it easy for foreign travellers to look them up in their phrase books. We use colloquial English to make it 'more friendly', more approachable and more difficult for others to understand. Come to think of it, I haven't written this book as an easy read for the overseas visitor and certainly not as the basis on which they should be educated in English grammar. The use of poor English isn't helped by the fact that so many overseas visitors who think they have learnt English, haven't learnt English at all. They have learnt that strange derivation which claims to be English, but which is really 'American', a different language altogether. Even my wretched spell checker and grammatical commentator courtesy of Microsoft, despite being set for the 'English (U.K.)' version, tries to Americanize most of what I write. (Or should that be Americanise?)

The fronts of trains don't always help the lost traveller, nor the platform boards for that matter. I don't need to know what the ultimate station is that the train is going to. I just need to know if it goes to my stop. Generally, this involves reverting to the board at the entrance to the platform, working out which is my east from my west, finding my destination on the list and then checking whether that is before or after the last stop of this particular train. On recollection, the Paris Metro was all in French and made no concessions to foreign travellers so why should I be concerned that we English are as bad?

What is meant on the front of a train by "Fast Amersham"? Is that supposed to be a place name? "Where do you live?" "Oh I live in Fast Amersham." Is it perhaps a description of Amersham? Is it either a speedy place or a place of questionable morals? Alternatively, is it in fact a description of the train? If it is this last one, does this mean that the train goes faster or does it mean that it doesn't stop at every stop and how do I know if it's my stop it won't stop at? How am I ever supposed to work out what to do? Tired from all these questions, I am now ready to get on a very slow train while I recover.

Then there are the useful signs on the trains themselves such as those on the Piccadilly Line trains to Heathrow. At one point these told me that Emirates did not fly to Abu Dhabi out of terminals 1,2 or 3 and that Iberia flew to everywhere but Bangkok out of those terminals, but if you wanted to go to Bangkok with Iberia you needed to go to terminal 4. Now where would I have been without knowing that? Of course, it did mean that I spent the whole of the rest of the day wondering why the Bangkok flight went from a different terminal to all the other Iberia flights and if the Abu Dhabi flight didn't go from terminals 1, 2 or 3 did that mean it went from 4 or 5 or that there wasn't one? If there wasn't one, why did they mention it in the first place? It's a bit like telling me the British Airways flight to the moon didn't go from terminals 1, 2 or 3. I would have assumed that meant that it went from terminal 4 or more likely 5. I could have turned up at terminal 5, asking for the moon flight, only to find I was in the wrong place.

'Ten Commandments'

1)   Thou shalt not eat any food that makes other passengers feel hungry.

2)   Thou shalt take up as little space as possible for yourself, your rucksack and your book.

3)   Thou shalt not sing, or whistle out of tune to your personal stereo.

4) Thou shalt turn the pages of your book at such a rate and in such a manner, that your fellow passengers are able to keep up and read all the words on the page.

5) Thou shalt not get your high-heeled shoes stuck in the escalator, particularly when inebriated.

6)   Thou shalt not consult the Tube map on your boxer shorts whilst wearing said garment.

7) Thou shalt not covet your neighbour's seat.

8)   Thou shalt honour the ticket machine and the ticket barrier.

9) Thou shalt not drip your umbrella in your neighbour's shoe.

10) Thou shalt not burp, fart or pick your nose in close proximity to your neighbour.

There are so many more that could be added, but there seems to be a precedent for ten.

TIME

'Tube Time' is a phenomenon in its own right. If you want any proof that the normal scientific laws cease to apply as you descend the escalators, you need look no further than one Tuesday. It seemed like a normal day. I may be a little glib with the use of the word normal, but the sun was shining and even the birds were croaking out the odd note or two through the fumes.

This particular Tuesday was my first real day of commuting in London. Prior to this, I had led a blissfully ignorant existence. I believed the traffic in Birmingham was as bad as commuting could get, unless you were to include getting stuck behind a herd of cows on the lane from Newton Abbot to Torquay, which is a very frustrating type of 'rush hour', not least for its unpredictability.

Back in London, I still had a spring in my step; I had not yet learnt to switch off all signs of intelligent life and emotion, in order to become 'Londonised'. I had not yet joined the 'carry a good pair of shoes to work in a bag' brigade, while wearing an old pair of running shoes for commuting. I was at heart still very much a provincial girl and as ill-equipped to deal with London as any new starter. The fact that I had noticed that the sun was shining and the birds were singing was a bit of a give-away on that front. Nevertheless, there I was, for the first time in my life, faced with a regular commute by Tube. I could not share this journey with a friend. Mine was the lone commuter existence.

The train 'arrivals and departures board' said one minute to my next train, or two minutes to the train after that. Ever the optimist, I thought things were going well. When train number one arrived, I wondered if there was an option of paying extra for breathing space. Instead, with another minute to wait for the next train, I let it go and waited for the next one. There was so much I had to learn. No one, until then, had introduced me to 'Tube time'. I discovered the hard way that there is a peculiar phenomenon by which, as soon as you descend below ground, time changes. I am told, by other bemused travellers, that it is caused by the earth's gravitational pull, meaning seconds and minutes become completely erratic and bear no resemblance to those experienced on the surface.

Somehow, back on that first morning, when moving up the board, from second train to 'the next train coming', that two minutes changed to seven minutes. In reality, this turned out to be eleven minutes according to the hands of my watch, which could themselves have been distorted. That train was also full. First time round, I had assumed that a train immediately following a full train stood a chance of having more free space, on account of it stopping at the same stations, where everyone would already have squeezed onto the previous train, just like buses. Although the theory of this is probably sound, I had no choice but to learn fast. I breathed in and forced my way into a corner, pressed up against the closing door. My conclusion, in the interests of survival, was, always force your way onto the first available train. There may not be another one and even if there is, it may be no better than the first.

It is important at this point to note that the commuters' definition of "Next train 4 minutes" reads – "Last time we checked, there was a train somewhere down the line and if you're lucky it might turn up soon." I am also assuming it is this phenomenon of 'Tube Time' that means the number of times it feels like your train is late, bears no relation to the number of times it is really late if you look at the official performance statistics. For the purpose of the official statistics, a train that is fourteen minutes late does not technically count as late. Remarkably, only those trains that are fifteen minutes or more behind time actually qualify as officially late.

If you were expecting your journey to take five minutes then an additional fourteen minutes can seem an awfully long time. This is compounded if your journey involves connections with a couple of train lines and you have to add all the fourteen minutes together. With three connections, you could be forty-two minutes late for your wedding and legitimately claim to your bride that you are on time. If you arranged to meet each other for a first date using different journeys by Tube, you may have missed each other altogether.

If you take it to the extreme, you may find you are lost underground for about a week and a half, just to complete a single journey across London. This may help to explain the number of stations that have statistics that show many hundreds more passengers entering in a day, than there are exiting on the same day. Somewhere below ground there is developing a whole community of lost passengers. Some of them are waiting for trains that never come; others have forgotten where they were going, because they have been there so long.

Whilst we are on the subject of lateness, what I have failed to work out is how the, all too regular, line closures are accounted for in the statistics. Is a train that never starts out, technically not late, or is there a category of 'infinite lateness'? Does Stephen Hawking need to explore the concept infinite non-existence? Through observation of the Tube, is it possible to understand the very beginnings of the creation of the Universe and if so, here is a project that could save the many millions of pounds being spent on research using the Large Hadron Collider deep below the ground under Geneva. Although, you have to acknowledge the scientists have the first bit right, they are at least working 'under ground'.

Another station phenomenon I have observed is platforms in different time zones. The second and minute hands match each other, tick by tock, but the hour hands are a full hour apart. Did I miss Charing Cross declaring partial independence from the rest of London and moving into the European time zone? Did I miss Greenwich declaring independence from British Summer Time? Failing either of those events, is this just a trick of engineering to reduce the number of trains that are late? Somewhere out there, is a commuter putting pen to paper to raise this very concern.

"Dear London Underground

I am writing to complain that my train from Charing Cross Underground Station yesterday, was no less than fifty minutes late.

Yours disgruntled of North of Watford"

To which, Transport For London might choose to reply;

"Dear disgruntled of North of Watford

We are very sorry that you were under the misapprehension that your train was late. If you had taken a moment to turn and look at the clock on the platform behind you, you would have observed that your train was ten minutes early.

Yours London Underground"

If the clocks in the offices of our esteemed employers ran on similar principles, it wouldn't be an issue, but alas by their clocks it is always you, the employee, who is late.

In 2005, travellers were invited to take part in a consultation on 'later weekend running of the Tube' in a press release from Transport for London. Was this questioning whether being several minutes late on a regular basis was enough? Were they enquiring whether passengers might like the opportunity to be ten minutes late on Saturdays and fifteen minutes on Sundays, rather than only seven minutes on a Monday? Sadly, what they wanted to know was whether travellers wanted the trains to run a whole hour later. This was quite literally the case, as the deal was that if the trains ran until an hour later at night they would have to start an hour later in the morning. In this way, the 8.06 train becomes the 9.06 and the 8.15 the 9.15 and so on. That's clear then. One hundred and forty thousand people wanted to use the Tube in the middle of the night but only fifty five thousand get up early. On the convenience side though, the fifty five thousand are probably going to work and the one hundred and forty thousand may have nothing better to do. To satisfy everyone, or no-one as the case may be, the conclusion was that they should run half an hour later on both Friday and Saturday and start an hour later on a Saturday morning to compensate. If you are using an out of date timetable you could have a long wait for the train first thing on a Saturday. Why Saturday? Well, here at least they have considered the fact that alternative transport is harder to find on a Sunday. Still no consolation if you wanted to use the Tube on a Saturday morning.

TOILETS IN LONDON

Those of you with large bladders may be oblivious to the problems outlined below. How, you might ask, are toilets relevant to life on the Tube? If you have ever needed one, you will already be painfully aware. Tube trains, to my knowledge, do not have toilets and contrary to the belief of some passengers, the platforms and corridors are not designed for this purpose either. Some stations do seem to have toilets, probably all of them if I looked properly, but whether you want to use them is a matter of personal choice. For my part, I would prefer not to. The toilets that for a small charge allow you to enter an automatically opened door and use a loo that, following use, is automatically cleaned are a wonderful invention, but they have their downsides. 1) They are never there when you need them. 2) There are not enough of them and waiting outside them, hopping from one leg to the other, gets you 'knowing looks' from anyone passing. 3) It is impossible to use them without the constant worry that the door is going to open automatically before you've finished, which would give you a full view of the world and the world a full view of you. 4) They always demand a coin that escapes you when you need it most or they already have a coin stuck fast in the slot, preventing their use.

One of these wonderful inventions was built as a

design statement and work of art, made out of one-way glass. It almost defies comment altogether. There you are, desperate to spend a penny and your only option is a toilet whose walls are made of glass. Much as you might have looked from the outside and convinced yourself it really was 'one way' glass, nerve would undoubtedly fail you once you got inside such a structure. Although the one in London was part of a 2003 Tate Britain exhibition, according to photos on the internet, a similar structure exists in Switzerland. This would be an occasion on which a room with a view is less than an ideal scenario. It is the sort of situation where you find, for no apparent reason, you can't 'go' at all and run the risk of the doors opening automatically before you're ready, but I guess as you already felt as though the whole world could see you, the door opening wouldn't make any difference.

The powers that be have now installed 'push button' door opening toilets on newer mainline trains. There are buttons with arrows for open and close, one with an 'L' for lock and one with an 'F' for flush. I get confused enough in lifts as to which arrow button to press. One way, you can be nice and let the people hurrying toward the lift get in and one way you accidentally close the door in someone's face. I don't need to make decisions of such magnitude whilst stressed. It must also be confusing if you don't speak English to work out what the 'L' and the 'F' might stand for. Unlocking the door when you meant to flush the loo could prove hazardous.

Meanwhile back at the Tube, it was late one evening and I had been for a night out on Tottenham Court Road. Well, not actually on the road itself more at a Salsa Bar there. I found I needed a loo as I walked back toward the Tube station. No way was I going to reach my destination without finding a toilet and there wasn't a single public toilet in sight. What's the next best thing, short of a 'dial a loo' service where the toilet comes to you and bearing in mind I'm female and a lamppost won't do? Fast Food Restaurants. You know the ones. You will realise in a minute why they may prefer not to have been named. I trotted (as best I could with my legs crossed) nonchalantly into this particular restaurant and straight to the loos. I did feel guilty about using their toilet and not even buying a bag of 'fries', but I worked on the principle I was probably in credit from the amount I've spent in there over the years. As I arrived at the door to the toilets, imagine my horror to be asked by the cleaner to wait whilst he removed the needles and blood. It was almost enough to make me reconsider the lamppost. So once again, I thank God for the inventor of the automatic opening public loo. A sensible approach would be to mark them all on the map and keep the map readily to hand. It is also worth staying in credit with fast food places. Don't knock them, one day you may need them.

I have also added to my education the reason why, in places such as the one I went to, they have resorted to installing strange blue lighting in their toilets. If that doesn't make sense to you – just don't ask – you wouldn't like the answer, but let's just say you can't see your veins in blue light.

UNANSWERED QUESTIONS

I am inquisitive and believe that in general terms a little bit of research is a good thing. I therefore leave you with some unanswered questions, which you are free to go away and research or write to the author with your best guess at the answers. This is not an exam and accuracy will not get you awarded full marks. I have already dealt with the question of why Che Guevara, an asthmatic Argentinean trained doctor, turned communist rebel, became a fashion icon amongst youth in the west, as well as remaining a hero in Cuba and this is not the place to explain the answer. It does freak people out when you pose the question though, so it's still worth a try.

However, try looking into one of these:
- Which stations are the most used and how many 'passengers per hour' pass through them?
- What is the earliest Tube start time and latest Tube finish time of any train running? (The correct answer should refer to the scheduled time as opposed to the actual time).
- How many deaths through natural causes occur, per year, on the Underground and what are the causes? Please exclude rats and other non-human animals.
- What are the highest and lowest numbers of

crimes committed per year at any Underground Station? And, what are the principal types of crime?
- How many Underground trains are there? And, what is the maximum number of trains that run at any point in time?
- Why does a bacon sandwich smell so good?
- Thinking about all of that should help to keep you out of trouble for a while.

Vandalism

Have you ever realised that you stop noticing the graffiti? However, you don't stop noticing before wondering who does the graffiti in the Tube tunnels. Is it some young people with time on their hands and no talent for art, who like to add the danger element to their profanity?

Graffiti is an area that Transport for London does not take lightly. I guess it's hard to differentiate between the good stuff that makes the journey more interesting and the graffiti the authorities describe as 'psychological mugging'. This wonderful term makes me wonder what the graffiti in question said that was so very bad. Whatever it was, it has been known to lead to criminal prosecutions and civil proceedings with damages of £3k being paid to 'make good' the 'artists' work. I find the term 'make good' an interesting one. Does it mean remove and reinstate to its original form, or does it mean turn the 'psychological mugging' into a work of art? In a year, it costs Transport for London £20m to 'make good' the graffiti on the Tube. That's an awful lot of bacon sandwiches that could be given out free to travellers instead.

Why don't Transport for London invite local artists to paint murals on the walls to brighten up the tunnels, or even the platforms? This could take the idea of 'Poems on the Underground' in a new direction. You could include a 'rehabilitation programme' for those who previously psychologically mugged commuters, getting the artists to paint beautiful graffiti instead. A whole new art form could be encouraged, attracting additional people to the Underground just to look at it. On reflection, if it made the Underground even busier, that may not be such a good idea.

Weather and Seasons

If you think you are now equipped to deal with Tube Time, then it's time to master the rigours of Tube Weather. It was early in my commuting days that I started to learn about 'Tube Weather', or the lack of it. There is no real weather, or even any clue to the real weather, within the Tube. If you board the train at a station close to where the train has come in from 'above ground' you may become aware of the diagonal splatters of raindrops across the windows. This is a sign that it's raining. However, within a couple of stations these will have blown away.

The existence of Tube Weather is another way in which the whole operation of the Underground runs contrary to the rules of science. You may leave the real world in darkness and emerge in bright sunshine, or, more depressingly, the opposite. You might leave a sunny day and arrive in rain and very occasionally leave in rain and emerge into sunshine.

There are one or two additional points that you should note. On days of heavy rain, the smell of people drying out on the Tube is not dissimilar to being thrust into a flock of damp sheep. Not that I have ever found myself thrust amongst a flock of damp sheep. Even without this experience, wet wool mixed with perspiration has a smell all of its own. In fact, on a crowded Tube with drenched sheep joining and leaving at regular intervals, it feels not unlike a human form of a sheep dip. All you need is for Transport for London to add a process of branding you as you enter the carriage and the sensation would be complete. You may also find on wet days that your fellow passenger's umbrella is steadily drip-drying into your shoe. This is enough to make your miserable existence complete.

I have spent more time than is healthy trying to decide whether this type of weather is worse to endure on the Tube than the opposite. You will be pleased to know I have also reached a conclusion. Do not travel by the Tube on hot summer days. If it is hot above ground, you can guarantee that this heat will be magnified as you descend. Forget 'heat rises'. With the Tube, heat successfully sinks. Once again, the laws of physics are defied, or maybe they just change and the earth's gravitational pull has the opposite effect on heat within the area of the Tube. On the other hand maybe it is linked to time and in fact 'Tube heat' does rise, but in the strange 'other world' of the Tube it does so more slowly, thereby allowing more heat to be generated before the last lot has risen. On a hot summer's day, it is better to get blisters walking, than to join many thousands of hot passengers, sweating uncontrollably in a confined space. I have been known to walk four or five miles across London and discovered some seedy streets in the process of finding shortcuts, rather than descend to the claustrophobic heat that is the Tube in summer. This is a problem with which Transport for London are familiar and for which they go to considerable lengths to provide assistance, including such considerations as free bottles of water, although to be fair this is at the expense of the bottled water company, as a marketing exercise.

Lovers Take up Less Space

In fairness to the Tube it is almost impossible to add air conditioning to the existing system, as the costs are prohibitive. I suspect instead that Transport for London have invested money with the Met Office in a special programme to create clouds over London, in order to keep the heat down, thus accounting for the complete absence of summer in most years.

There are ways that it is possible to observe the changing seasons when using the Tube. This is not because you can see the trees coming into leaf, or the flowers into bud, nor because of the sunshine on your face. No, the changing seasons on the Tube can be observed as follows:

- January – Excessive numbers of large bags marked 'SALE' and overcrowding at times other than rush hour.
- Easter – Too many children and families looking as though they are enjoying the experience. However, the introduction of free travel on 'off peak' times for children, with up to four accompanying any one adult, makes this a serious risk at any time of year.
- June – Excessive numbers of European students hitting you as they turn round forgetting they are wearing a backpack. I am presuming they have forgotten. This may just be a ploy to see how many English people they can hit and get away with it.
- July – A dire combination of hot commuters, hot but suitably (or in some cases – barely) dressed tourists and excessive bags marked 'SALE'.
- August – Many loud voiced Americans discussing our 'quaint' sights and thinking the only place in England outside London is called Stratford. (I wonder how many foreigners are confused by the fact that there is

a Stratford in London too.)

- October – All passengers obliged to look windswept, wet and miserable. The overpowering smell of wet wool. You only need to panic if the smell is coming from a live sheep on the Tube. The best form of defence on such occasions is to look happy. It freaks out your fellow passengers.
- December – Increased incidence of drunkenness, combined with excessive bags with Christmas designs, children, thick coats that take up more space and wet umbrellas. All in all, a month not to be recommended to the faint hearted.

There is also one type of weather that the Tube creates all on its own and that is wind. Laws of physics state that 'An approaching train displaces a considerable volume of air on arriving at a station'. This air develops cyclonic properties in order to rearrange passengers' neatly brushed hair and any loose papers they may be carrying. When travelling by Tube, it is advisable for men and women alike to use excessive quantities of hairspray, carry a comb or be prepared to look a mess. I have always gone with the latter option. It is also advisable to keep all loose papers well under control. Chasing your private correspondence down the platform is both embarrassing and difficult. Retrieving them from electrified lines or from under trains is dangerous and wherever they have been in the meantime it is unlikely that you are going to want to hold them afterwards (not without disposable gloves).

Descending the escalator wearing a full circle skirt is also not advisable for the same reason of 'wind', particularly if that skirt is one made of light, easily blown material. If choosing not to follow this advice please remember to wear good, clean underwear, or at the very least 'some' underwear. From observing my fellow travellers, this advice is equally levelled at men choosing to wear a full circle skirt, as it is the women who do so. If you have no other underwear, this may be a good point to purchase a pair of boxer shorts sporting the map of the Tube from the London Transport Museum Shop. This would have the added advantage of providing something to consult at the points you don't know what connection you need for your journey. It is advisable to do this in private and not in the middle of the carriage, as having a lot of tourists working out their journeys while pointing rather closely at your boxer shorts may not be considered in the best of taste, particularly if you are wearing them at the time. For this purpose, you might find the socks marginally more sociable with the added advantage that removing your shoes to consult them may clear the carriage of passengers and provide you with more space.

Should you choose to ignore the advice on when not to travel, you will need to adopt suitable survival techniques. These may include air-conditioned underwear in summer or no underwear as long as you are not wearing a full circle skirt. On rainy days an all in one wetsuit will prevent the dripping of people's umbrellas proving annoying. On windy days, or in fact any Tube travelling day, a toupee or wig is ill advised, whereas a headscarf might prove useful. Feeling physically cold is unlikely to be a problem with lots of warm sweaty bodies to be crammed against, however the germ spread variety of cold is likely to prevail.

Sneezing over your fellow passengers, despite it seeming to be the norm, is not considered an acceptable practice, particularly if it is a very wet type of sneeze. In addition to that, it was never very pleasant to find myself stood near the man that insisted on clearing his nasal passages over the track, without a handkerchief.

It is important to remember that every cloud has a bit of a shiny edge and there are at least three plus points to travelling by Tube in extreme weather. Firstly, you are unlikely to get sunburnt. Secondly, you are unlikely to get soaked while waiting for the train and no car is going to drive deliberately through a puddle to soak you from head to toe. Finally, in very windy weather it is unlikely that trees or leaves will prove obstacles to the trains unless you are travelling on underground lines that also go overground.

What does the future hold for Tube Weather? In this age of global warming, it is important to think of the implications for the phenomenon. The Tube when compared to many methods of transport is environmentally friendly, with efforts for improvement being made all the time. Will 'Tube Weather' become more extreme with the progression of global warming? Not only does the prospect of more rainfall not augur well for the 'wet sheep' smell, but also greater extremes of temperature will aggravate any summer journeys and that is before you ask the question 'how high would sea level have to rise before the tunnels started to flood?'

WHAT IF?

The Tube can be a very odd place, but what if it didn't stop there? (What if the trains didn't stop at all? This might present a different set of questions.) We've already proved that the laws of science are distorted as you go below ground. What if you take the idea of distortion one step further? There are so many possibilities.

Imagine for a moment that the Tube might be like the children's television programme Mr Benn. In that programme, Mr Benn ends up wearing different clothes and then does something exciting, instead of his normal, routine, bowler hatted life. Just supposing that instead of a change of clothing, by entering the Underground, this was enough for you to become a different person. Some of us might settle for the same person, only nicer, or better looking. You could find yourself inside the mind of someone you knew. Is there anyone that you wonder what's going on inside their heads? Imagine being able to find out first hand, rather than being fobbed off with "Oh nothing," when you ask them the question, "What are you thinking?" You might be alarmed and find there is nothing going on in there, or you might find a miniature football match has just run into extra time, or worse, golf.

What if going below ground took you into another dimension? In this other world it may be possible that things look the same and you are the same person, however, the normal patterns of behaviour might have changed. In this world, it might be acceptable to turn round, hitting someone with your rucksack and to repeat this activity at twenty second intervals as you check whether the 'next train' information board has been updated. Alternatively, perhaps it is a world in which clearing your throat and spitting it out on the track is considered ok, or even normal. On the other hand, maybe, in this world pushing old people out of the way, in order to get a seat, is also normal. Maybe in this other world it would be usual for trains to be cancelled or late. Maybe you wouldn't think anything of the lights going out repeatedly while you were travelling. Maybe it is a world where all these things happen, but even when they do, the people faced with the problems manage to stay smiling and good tempered and even say hello to their fellow passengers: - so many possibilities.

An alternative 'What If?' would be to imagine that the act of going below ground made you somebody else, with a different life. Who would you be? Now being realistic, you will still need to be someone who would travel by Tube, so finding yourself as an 'A list' celebrity is probably not an option, unless you are one who demonstrates that you haven't lost touch with your roots. Or should that be routes?

There is always the possibility of entering the Tube and still being you, but entering a different time in history. Maybe it is when you go back above ground, the other end of your journey, that the time change would kick in. Set off in 2011 and arrive in 2015 – of course, with delays and the possibility of catching the wrong train that is always a possibility. How about if it worked the other way and you set off in 2011 and arrived in 1666. You could get an eyewitness report of the Great Fire of London, but then you might have a bit of a problem trying to get back. You can just imagine going up to ask a local "Excuse me Mr Pepys where will I find the nearest Tube Station?" Never mind trying to explain the Underground, your first problem would be to explain what a train was without being locked up for being mad. "Well it's this large wagon made out of metal with an engine powered by electricity." "Where in the story did I lose you? Electricity, engine? Oh, you want me to go back to metal wagon. Right!" You may of course not have got this far given that your clothes would have given you away as an alien and you would already have stood out trying to get a mobile phone signal.

What if time stayed the same, but the place changed? What if the process of getting into an underground train was as normal, but somewhere as you entered the tunnel, the train was transported to another underground system, somewhere else in the world? Now let's be honest here, one Tube tunnel looks much the same as another Tube tunnel. How do you know it couldn't happen? This would be a sort of 'parallel world' of the Underground. You might get on at Oxford Circus and expect to go to Covent Garden, intending to change at Holborn just two stops along the Central Line. You set off as normal and even pass through Tottenham Court Road without incident, but then when you get out of the carriage at the next stop, it seems to be San Giovanni station on the Metro Linea 'A' in Rome. Not only are you now in the wrong place, but you can't change to a different line as it isn't even an intersection. You also have the added worry that you haven't got your passport. Your next step is to go to the other platform and try to catch the train back, but you come out at the Champs Elysees Clemenceau station on line 1 in Paris and if you had stayed on for another three stops you could have got out at the Louvre. If you think that getting to Mornington Crescent is bad when playing rule 56, (if you are unfamiliar with the game there are many useful internet sites that can be visited), then you should try getting back to Covent Garden from the Champs Elysees in less than four changes.

Although there would be some difficulties if this happened, you do have to wonder if the Rome stop might have presented an interesting opportunity for increasing the number of people who have paired off in the carriage through your dating scheme. There is nothing like a man with brown eyes and a dark complexion to convince the women passengers that it's worth taking a risk. If you add to that an Italian accent, it could work wonders.

Maybe the European angle is a little unlikely, but what if you come out at the right place, you are the right person, it is the right date but in the meantime, history has taken a different course. Maybe Britain is not a democracy and an oppressive, extremist government is ruling the country. Maybe it is a Big Brother state in which your every movement is watched and you have precious little freedom. Alternatively, European history has taken a different course and we are now one federal Europe, with French as the first language. A European president has replaced the Queen and fluffy white Bichon Frisés have replaced the Buckingham Palace Corgis. You now have to ask yourself whether you would rather that outcome or the alternative in which we are now the fifty-fourth state of the USA, others having got there before us. If we went for the US option at least there might now be a baseball team called the 'Buckingham Palace Corgis'.

However, let us for a moment consider what happens if the changes are a little less pronounced. All these options just add greater possibilities to the dating agency you've set up. If all the passengers around you aren't who they normally are in their lives above ground, there are endless possibilities of getting them together below ground, to take up less space. It's worth a thought. This becomes a problem if they were travelling together with someone when the changes took place. In this 'other life' they may not be prepared to split up from their original partner and be paired with other passengers, who, in your opinion, would have been more suitable for them. If they both paired off with unattached people in the carriage, you could make two couples instead of one. More often than not people seem to be prepared to pair off with the most unlikely matches and rarely consider the people to whom they are best suited. If this is the case then you have your work cut out.

From a survival point of view, letting your imagination run free and starting to believe any of this, may be enough to carry you through many Tube journeys. So who do you fancy being today? Your choice could be anyone from Casanova to the Pope, Mata Hari to Mother Teresa, or for that matter Windy Miller to Bart Simpson. Let your fantasies run wild. Not too wild or you may find yourself spending the rest of the day behind bars. (That is bars of the police variety, rather than the one in your imagination with a warm fire and a cold pint. As this is Britain, that should perhaps read 'a cold fire and a warm pint'.) Once you're released from police custody, you may also find yourself facing the divorce courts, which is probably a greater peril, though it may provide more time to spend in bars, with a warm fire and a cold pint.

X - RATED

There is a time and a place for everything and this was neither the time nor the place. It was about eleven o' clock at night, I'd left a Christmas Party, in the hope of getting a cab back to my hotel. I walked out, from the little side road, onto Holborn, with the intention of hailing a cab.

Holborn has always struck me as a very nice area. An area you can find yourself thinking of London's grander days. An area where you think that hailing a cab might be commonplace.

If you have ever tried getting a cab in London, at night, you will know that I was being a little naïve thinking that even that early in the evening it might be easy. I have never quite mastered the technique of stopping a cab at any time of day. It's a little like trying to catch a cat. If you find them waiting locked in a cat basket, they are no trouble at all, but just try to catch one out in the wild. It doesn't matter which angle you try to creep up on it from, it is impossible. Just as you are about to pounce, it trots off in the other direction without even looking at you. And so it is with cabs in London.

When I try to catch a cab, if I look up the road, the best that happens is a cab comes down the road while my back is turned. If I switch my head from side to side, not only do I resemble a nodding dog, but no cab appears from either direction. There are times of night and places in London where cabs regularly set people down and you can pick a taxi up quite easily. I never seem to be in one of those places and as far as I know, Holborn is not one of them.

There I stood, on the edge of the pavement, looking up and down the road, but to no avail. I was looking around me to make sure I wasn't about to be mugged as I waited. I looked up the road. I looked down the road. I looked quickly in both directions in case there was a cab moving at speed. Then I looked around me and down at the pavement. It wasn't that I was expecting to find a cab on the pavement, but you can never be too certain.

I thought I had seen everything, well not literally you understand, but there are some things you just do not expect. To my horror, I was standing right next to a couple in the midst of what went way beyond a passionate embrace, necessitating the removal of certain items of clothing, right there on the pavement. They were for the most part still clothed, but that wasn't the point. I felt like I had booked front seats to an '18' rated movie. There I was, trying to call a cab. What was I supposed to do? Should I pretend I couldn't see and continue to hope a cab would come to my rescue? Or should I move on, out of sight?

I'm not a great fan of taking the Tube when travelling alone at night and having a vivid imagination doesn't make it a more pleasant experience. But that was not a normal situation, what would you have done? Short of holding up score cards awarding them marks out of ten for style and performance, I didn't much fancy staying where I was. The Tube seemed like a good idea. I moved briskly along the pavement and disappeared into the

Tube. Despite my misgivings, as I went underground, I didn't look back.

As I moved through the tunnel with its flickering lights and its smell of stale urine, I did wonder whether I had made the right decision or whether I would have been better to stay to watch. I had the stark choice of a live '18' rated movie 'containing scenes of a explicit sexual nature' above ground, or a live '18' rated movie, 'containing scenes of a violent and horrific nature' (in my head if not in reality), below ground – tough call. In the embarrassing moments it took to make my decision, I did think that given how cold it was, it couldn't be that long before they left. Being an optimist, I was also clinging to the thought that at any moment a cab would arrive.

I did also start to wonder whether science was playing a part. If the magnetism of a Tube station has the same polarity as a London cab, it would prevent the cab from coming within a certain radius. There, you'd never thought of that before had you? Not being able to get a cab starts to make more sense in the light of that. This could explain why no transport strategy ever seems to work. Maybe all transport has the same polarity and therefore can never meet up.

Whatever else I might say; the Tube is an easy method of transport. You turn up, without booking, buy a ticket at a known, fixed price and within a matter of minutes, escalators and all other variable factors being equal, you are on a train heading for your destination. You don't have to go through passport control; you don't go through customs and break into a nervous sweat, even when the most exciting thing you're carrying is a bag of dirty clothes. You don't get searched by some stranger when you invariably set off the metal detector and you don't have to wait in the rain (unless it is an above ground Underground station). You don't have to check in and be at the gate at least 40 minutes before the train leaves and you don't find that you've gone to Green Park and your luggage has gone to Richmond. If you miss the particular train you thought you were going to catch, no one tries to charge you a premium to get on another one, or if you turn up early, no one tells you that you cannot travel until your originally intended time. All in all the Underground provides an amazingly efficient and good value travel service, however…

YOGA'S BENEFITS FOR SECURING CARRIAGE SPACE

If the discontinuity of time doesn't convince you that you are dealing with something very 'other worldly' just look at carriage space. The Guinness Book of Records is renowned for all the records of how many people you can get into a...Mini / phone box / public toilet etc, but what about a Tube carriage? Don't you think it is incredible that an apparently full carriage arriving at a station and not discharging more than one or two passengers, is then able, as if by magic, to accommodate a further 25 people waiting on the platform? There seems to be a real knack of passengers fitting into every available corner; a skill I have never mastered. Can children, growing up in London, choose it as a curriculum option? It would be one of the more useful GCSE subjects and should be, perhaps, right up there with literacy and numeracy for entering the workforce in London. Standing back and watching the experts getting onto a packed carriage is a sight to behold. First, they line themselves up with one of the sets of doors (double doors seem to be more popular, so the real specialists opt for the single ones on the end). They stand approximately three paces back from the edge of the platform, (this bit is very clever because they can disguise what they're doing by making it look as though they are politely waiting for the disembarking passengers to 'alight'). Then at the last moment, the experts hurl themselves forward and merge with the people already in the carriage. If only my attempts to copy them were as successful. For me it is the case that I launch myself at the carriage, just as someone swings a rucksack round at face height and I encounter it with an embarrassing 'thwack'. Even if I have no breathing space, at least I'm too dazed for the rest of the journey to notice.

You may want to provide exercises in the above tactics as part of your dating agency 'getting to know you' sessions). It's a bit like speed dating, but on a physical basis. The upside of this is that when you start your relationship with someone on such an intimate basis, there is no point becoming coy later on. The downside would be following my method, that you are in no position to start a relationship, intimate or otherwise.

Included in the notes on Tube etiquette on the Transport for London website is a great little request that 'when sitting – please don't spread your legs' and I don't think at this point they are solely directing it at the lovers in the corner of the carriage.

This brings us to the next consideration. When viewing the limited space available, it's useful to build this into your exercise programme. Undertaking step-aerobics or circuit training as part of your daily commute may prove a little difficult. Although the dash between platforms may resemble some aspects of circuit training, other aspects of this type of exercise are not the best choice to make. Undertaking squat thrusts against tightly packed commuters can also get you arrested. For those of you who are short of time, or too stingy to pay money to a gym you never attend, there are ways of improving your

Lovers Take up Less Space

fitness and making better use of carriage space at the same time. Try yoga, or if you are more up-to-date 'pilates'. This has at least two advantages. It will enable you to become so supple that when necessary, you can wrap your legs round your neck as you hang from the overhanging wrist supports. In addition to this you will also be able to hold your breath long enough to avoid needing to breathe when there is no space available. Meditating in this position can have the added advantage of allowing you to rise above the stress and anguish of peak time travelling. It may also elicit phone numbers from strange men. This may or may not be seen as an advantage. Your view may of course also depend on whether you are a man or a woman hanging from a wrist support with your legs round your neck and whether you have inadvertently or deliberately wrapped them round someone else's neck.

In Tokyo, special carriages are set aside in rush hour for women and children. This may involve a different approach to the clothes you choose to wear in the morning, if for example as a man you believe these carriages will be less congested, this may justify going to work in a skirt and jacket instead of your usual trousers. This works more easily if you have a broad-minded employer or if you can secure enough room on the Tube to carry a change of clothing. It may also mean that you need to take a different approach to the creation of your dating agency.

There has been a suggestion on the Tube that pregnant women wear a 'baby on board' sticker. This leads to many possibilities. How many men will see if they can get away with a 'baby on board' sticker? Will a black market develop in the stickers and what price will they be traded at? Will E-bay allow them to be auctioned?

Are these stickers just a natural consequence of the dating agency or of the lovers in the corner? How do you ensure that these genuinely worthy women are given the treatment they deserve and how do you ensure that the project isn't marred by the spin off opportunities? Is this just the first of many stickers? It could be followed with: 'Bad back from too much sex', (although perhaps not immediately after pregnancy.) 'I'm old really, I just don't look my age' and then for those who feel they have no good justification, but would like to sit down anyway, you could have 'Feet aching from too much shopping' and then my favourite 'Too lazy to stand up'.

Of course finding a seat is no guarantee that your troubles have come to an end. I had just sat myself down and was happily tucking into a ginger biscuit, when a small boy with red hair came and peered at me. I thought he wanted a biscuit until he grumpily said to his mum "I wanted to sit there." "Well sit on that one," she said, pointing to the next seat, which neighboured where his brother was sitting. "But I want to sit on that one. I want to sit there, that's my seat." Tyler or Taylor or whatever his name was, started to get grumpy about everything and declared he didn't like me. I could assure him, just at that moment I didn't like him either. Instead I was very English and carried on with what I was doing, pretending not to notice him. If I had been my mother, I would by now have engaged him in conversation and distracted his attention from his bad mood, however being me I thought about moving seat, but decided it was more fun to stay where I was. However, I did hope sincerely that he wasn't travelling far in the same direction. His parents were getting increasingly embarrassed by his pointing and announcing more loudly that he hated me. I was so tempted to wait for the next time he did it and to say, "Listen, kid. I don't think you're so wonderful". That would have stopped him in his tracks. However, I looked at his dad and decided he may not be the type of person who would appreciate me getting my own back on his thug of a son.

Space on the Tube is not just about people. There is the luggage. It is quite common to find people moving suitcases that are bigger than they are. Once they have negotiated dragging it down the stairs or escalator they then have to force their way into a carriage to enable them to drop it down on several peoples' feet. You can only marvel at the prospect of how they plan to get it up the stairs at the other end, as you rub your sore foot, which you have tortuously removed from below the case. In these circumstances, scowling at them seems to serve little purpose, as in general people crazy enough to carry that amount of luggage on a crowded train appear to be oblivious to the impact of their actions.

Being London, even screaming is likely to bring you little attention. Screaming may however cause your fellow passengers to inch a little bit away if they can, which in itself can be useful. What you can do is spend your journey wondering what they might be carrying. Are they going on a long holiday, or a short holiday, but couldn't decide what to wear and so have packed their entire wardrobe. When do any of us women ever need as many clothes as we pack? Men on the other hand could benefit, on occasions, from packing one or two more items.

Meanwhile back on the Tube. Has the person with the large suitcase left home and taken all their worldly belongings with them? Have they just robbed a bank and are now using the Tube as an inconspicuous getaway vehicle? Suitcases are only one type of luggage that causes a problem. There are always people with more shopping bags than seem to be sensible. The challenge of one person trying to manage fifteen carrier bags has always been something that I have shied away from, let alone when combining it with Tube travel. Do the people carrying this number of bags put them under their legs and as far out of the way as possible? No. In general, they take up extra seats for their beloved shopping, leaving other passengers to stand in awe.

It has always seemed a nonsense that the main place designed for putting larger luggage is the doorway. There is nothing like making it easy for people to get on and off the train and this is nothing like making it easier for people to get on and off the train.

ZONES

For the purpose of the Tube, London consists of a number of concentric circles, although I use the term circle generously. This enables you to buy a ticket covering just part of the great city. For most people this would be Zone 1 or Zones 1 and 2 as this covers central London and most lines connect to each other in those zones, making it possible to get to all places around this area without trespassing on Zone 3. If you look further afield, a pass covering Zones 5 and 6 makes it theoretically possible to get from Epping to Heathrow, both being in the outer zones at opposite corners of London. Life was never this straightforward. In reality, this journey would mean crossing the other zones, as no train goes round the edge.

Even going from Barkingside to Becontree, not that far apart (4.8miles) and both in zone 5 can only be achieved by going into Zone 3 and out again. Better still, to travel from West Ruislip to Ickenham both in Zone 6 (0.7 miles apart) also means going via Zone 3 – in fairness this is one that would be quicker to walk, but you get my point.

Zones are there to trip you up, if you aren't that familiar with London. Who decided on the zones and what was the basis of the decision? In certain parts, maybe it was the likelihood of wanting to do a certain route; in others, maybe it was ability to pay. Are the residents of Woodford and Loughton perhaps more affluent? They are however, not so affluent that they wouldn't use a Tube. Why there in particular? You may well ask. Woodford and Loughton are both 'Central Line' stations, just two stops apart, a distance of 3.2 miles by road and yet one is in Zone 4 and one is in Zone 6, a 3-zone pass would be required.

Then of course, there is the Metropolitan Line. This project clearly got too ambitious and Zones 1 to 6 were not considered adequate. What do the powers that be do then? Did they add Zones 7, 8 and 9? No, that would have been way too obvious. Although now they have seen the light and called them 7, 8 and 9, to begin with you ran into Zones A, B, C and D. Who would be a foreigner in London? I wonder what made them go for letters and what blinding revelation helped them to see the lunacy of their ways. In their defence, this line takes you a whole 27 miles away from Central London. Once you get this far out, it should perhaps be known as 'The Nowhere Near London Underground'.

In reality, London has 'different types of traveller' zones. You can tell by how the traveller is dressed whether they are going to a theatre, to work in The City, shopping, or to museums and galleries. Perhaps tickets should be zoned by activity or by type of traveller. This would also have the advantage of allowing extra to be charged for small children and lovers who should pay more for the fact that they are still able to enjoy using the Tube while the rest of us suffer.

Tube Dictionary

Advertising – posters appearing repeatedly around trains or stations for things you a) can not afford b) already have, but paid more for c) would be too embarrassed to ask for anyway d) will find out later are no longer available. Alternatively, it is the dubious pastime of actors entering trains pretending they can't live without the latest washing powder, in the hope, of the manufacturers, that you will be gullible enough to listen to them.

Air-conditioning – This is something that for the most part you can only dream of when on a platform, underground. Sadly, according to the Transport for London web site information, most of the lines are too deep below ground to make the introduction of air conditioning a remote possibility in the near future. However, it is something which is being introduced on the trains themselves, with the first air-conditioned trains now in full operation. Eventually these trains will run on 40% of the Underground. Which probably means your journey will be on the other 60%.

Alighting – A peculiar term in common parlance when using trains and conjuring up an image of an event that took place over a hundred years ago. Somehow, it gives rise to thoughts of a far more genteel pastime than travelling by Tube.

Announcements – Grunts and fuzzy noises, that represent the almost mute, charade, version of useful messages.

Bacon Sandwich – one of many items it is cruel to fellow passengers to eat on the Tube, unless enough fresh bacon sandwiches are being provided for the whole carriage.

Bakerloo Line – unattractive brown coloured line that passes both Baker Street and Waterloo. I think this is a missed opportunity. What about renaming it the Elephant Circus Line – on account of it going to Elephant and Castle and passing through both Oxford Circus and Piccadilly Circus.

Bank – This is the deepest station underground in Inner London at 136 feet. Given that it is the 'London Underground', with no distinction between 'inner' and 'outer', one can only assume that Bank was having a lack of self-confidence and that announcing this fact was designed to boost its self-esteem. The real deepest station is Hampstead, which, clearly, is part of the 'Outer London' Underground at 192 feet.

British tourists – These are the grumpy passengers, still displaying signs of body language and carrying a map.

Business travellers (non-London) – grumpy passengers, still displaying signs of body language, looking flustered and attempting to disguise the map clutched on the inside of their briefcase. Generally found in queues on a Monday morning trying to buy a ticket. Given the request by Transport for London not to do this, it is probably the most daring thing they will do all week.

Cancelled – Term used to mean your travel plans are being disrupted and you are likely to be late for work. It also means the next train will have twice the normal number of people crammed inside, to compensate.

Carriage – This is a section of the train with more people than seats during any vaguely popular travel period. Surprisingly, as far as I can see, there seem to be no maximum number of passengers that a carriage can legally carry. This is a point on which I hope I am wrong, but whatever the answer there appears to be no one to prevent more than that number boarding the train.

Central Line – Tube line going through the centre of London to all the places you need to go to, but with carriages that are impossible to squeeze onto unless travelling at very off-peak times. Strangely, for its name, this line stretches to West Ruislip in the west (zone 6) and to Epping in the east (also zone 6). To confuse matters further there is no station called Central. However, there is an odd little loop, which could make you think you have entered TV land, including Chigwell and Grange Hill, but no Walford East.

Change – A term used to mean 'alight' here and walk miles through smelly tunnels in order to catch another Tube that will just be leaving the platform as you approach. Alternatively, it may be more in the sense of the television series Mr Benn and you will in fact come out as the same person, but living a completely different life and wearing very strange clothes. (For some passengers this may have been how they entered the Tube, in which case, continue as you were.)

Children – small passengers who look happy, up to the point they get trodden under foot in an attempt to a) get on the train b) get a seat – depending on time of day. After being trodden on, they have the tendency to wail loudly and convince the whole carriage that I am a bad person for having stood on them. These passengers are likely to be discovered finding it hard to resist the urge to push or pull the 'Emergency Stop' button but with little means to pay the penalty fine for so doing.

Circle Line – Tube line going in a 'circle' around London that appeared, while I was travelling, to break down on a regular basis. For the most part, this line seems completely useless, as it doesn't go anywhere not served by another line. Useful if you want to spend the day going round and round in circles and not get off anywhere. To reduce the cost of this process it falls entirely in Zone 1.

Commuters –These tired, worn-out looking people use the Tube on a regular basis.

Delayed – Term meaning you're going to be late for work and the train will be packed. Given the fact that the train is delayed, any regular notices that appear on the board cease to have meaning. Do not for example measure 'Next train 4 minutes' against any watch or clock. Even with the laws of physics affecting the clocks on the Tube, you are still unlikely to find one that will accurately match the length of time to the next train. Welcome once again to the Tubelight Zone.

District Line – for the most part the Circle Line in disguise, except where it catches you unawares by shooting off in directions you did not have in mind going (being under the misapprehension that you were on a Circle Line train). I don't even understand the logic of all the different offshoots coming under one name. You wonder whether they couldn't be bothered to give new names for the offshoots and so just put them under the umbrella of 'District'. It strikes me the name Misfit Line would be a more embracing term. Question, "What do Ealing Broadway, Wimbledon, Richmond, Kensington (Olympia), Edgware Road and Upminster have in common?" Answer, "They are all at the end of the District Line". Come on, how many ends can one line have?

Docklands Light Railway – Now strictly speaking I don't think this counts as the Tube. Like the District Line, it has many ends but unlike the District Line, it doesn't call itself a 'Line' so I don't take issue with it. I haven't used it in rush hour, but grudgingly I have to say I quite enjoyed using it during the daytime. This may of course be because it was a) above ground b) relatively new. Maybe it is just that any railway going to places called 'Mudchute' and 'Pudding Mill Lane' on the one hand and 'East India' and 'Cyprus' on the other, has to have something going for it. For the benefit of the American tourists, it even goes to Stratford.

East – This is a direction commonly seen on signs, particularly with regard to one side of the road or the other. Rarely shown in conjunction with any clue to help you work out which one you wanted, or any indication of which way is 'north'. You may think that 'north' is obvious from the fact that it is signposting East, but they cleverly add twists and turns to the steps leading out from the Tube in order to completely confuse you.

East London Line –This was a short line as part of the Underground network, which, despite its length, still provided grounds for confusion. It went from Shoreditch to New Cross. However, for the unsuspecting traveller it forked and also ended at New Cross Gate. If that wasn't confusing enough, it now appears as part of the Overground network and does from New Cross to Canonbury, passing Shoreditch on route. The end to New Cross Gate now merely passes through it on its way to West Croydon.

Escalators – These are overcrowded moving walkways that are out of order on those occasions that you have most to carry, except, annoyingly, when accompanied by your pet giraffe (see section on pets). They are also noted for their handrails moving at a different speed from the walkway, leading to a peculiar stretching of the arm if firmly gripped. They have existed since 1911 and Waterloo can boast an incredible 25 of them and 2 separate passenger conveyors. Given that escalators convey passengers, what is a passenger conveyor? Perhaps, instead of escalators they should all be referred to as 'passenger conveyors' with the distinction being whether they are flat or with a gradient. Waterloo could then boast 27 passenger conveyors including 25 that deal with sharp inclines.

Exit – These are arrow signs often pointing in both directions to let you know how to get out. They are not usually accompanied by enough information for you to leave by the right one to reach your preferred destination.

Favourite station name – This definitely has to be Mudchute, with Pudding Mill Lane a close second. Although calling the station you arrived at from France 'Waterloo' also appealed to my sense of humour, until the

Eurostar moved to St Pancras.

Final station – Mysterious place to be found at both ends of every line. "This is the final station. This train terminates here. Please take all your belongings with you when leaving the train."

Food outlets –These are not quite as the name suggests. They are not little vents from which food spontaneously pours onto the platform. They are little kiosks from which you can be enticed to inflict pain on your fellow passengers by carrying hot coffee or ketchup laden bacon sandwiches.

Foreigners – These are passengers who look happy. Whether this is down to being foreign, travelling on the Tube, or carrying a rucksack is far from clear.

Gap (The) –This is the thing to be avoided at all costs. In the more explicit announcements, it is made clear that the particular Gap to avoid is the one between the train and the platform. Where this is not made clear, feel free to imagine the many types of gap you may be best to avoid. This should definitely not include the stores of the same name who sell some very practical clothing for dealing with life on the Tube and any suggestion that the announcements are discouraging you from visiting those wonderful establishments must be vigorously denied.

Ghost platform – A platform that doesn't exist, except it does. It is still there, just not in use anymore. It has been sidelined by the vagaries of the Tube line changing course.

Ghost station – As with a ghost platform, a ghost station is a 'has-been'. It is a relic of another time. It is a station that was once in use but has now been made redundant in favour of less convenient locations.

Hammersmith and City Line – More correctly this is in fact the Hammersmith to Barking Line. It does pass through The City of London but there is no actual place called City and that is certainly not its end point. It only runs on its own from Hammersmith to Royal Oak and from there onwards, shares its route with the Circle and District Lines. To add to confusion, whereas on the south side of London, the District Line is the same route as the Circle Line, the Hammersmith and City Line shares with the Circle Line to the north and only shares with the District Line after leaving the Circle Line. That's clear then.

Hampstead – This is the deepest station underground at 192 feet.

Harry Beck – He is the man who was responsible for designing a map that represents the Underground in the efficient manner of an electrical diagram, but completely confuses me.

Holly Bush Hill, Hampstead – ironically for a hill, this is the deepest point below ground at 221 feet. I'm guessing the land goes up rather than the line dips down, but it could prove an interesting journey if there were sudden dips and just think of the possibilities for a Playstation game. You could have a whole game around trying to negotiate your trains around the stations and stop at the right points to squeeze all your passengers in.

Incident – This is a euphemism for events that they don't want to tell you the truth about. Whatever has actually occurred, if you have an imagination like mine, it is almost certain that, as a result of the announcement, you will imagine something far worse than the reality of the situation.

Jubilee Line – Line running from Stanmore to Stratford. At no point does it pass through any place called Jubilee. As it does take an alternative route from Baker Street to Waterloo to the one taken by the Bakerloo Line, I would like to rename it the Bakerloo Mark II Line just to add to confusion. Presumably, this was called the Jubilee line to celebrate Queen Elizabeth ll's silver jubilee in 1977. However, as it was opened in 1979, it should have been called 'The Two Years After Jubilee Line' or TYAJL for short.

Late – Term regularly applied to trains. In general parlance this would mean running at a time after the one scheduled. In Tube terminology, this may vary according to the settings of the clocks and may in fact mean running ahead of the schedule by some Underground time-pieces. Fundamentally, it relates to the Tube not being there at the point you expect. However, if it is less than fifteen minutes after the appointed time, it is technically still on time and not classified as late. Try that on your boss.

Line – This is the descriptive name given to a series of stations along the same track and visited by the same train. However, for confusion see District Line.

Lovers - Couple entwined around each other in the corner of the carriage, who, perversely, seem to enjoy travelling by Tube and have no idea that there is an overcrowding problem.

Luggage – Many and varied items forming a barricade around the entrance and exit to the carriage, ensuring passengers are met by an 'obstacle course challenge', in order not to miss their stop.

Map (Underground) – This is a strangely deformed representation of places around London, bearing little resemblance to my perception of reality, except in so far as it demonstrates which places connect to each other. The whole concepts of distance and relative position above ground are surprisingly of little consequence to Harry Beck's 'Map'. I seem to remember in my school days I was marked down in Geography when I took this approach with maps.

Maximum – A statistic that is apparently non-existent when it comes to passengers within a Tube carriage.

Metro – name used in some parts of the world for the Tube or Underground. To add to confusion in London this is the name of a free newspaper, so the unsuspecting non-local traveller asking, "Where will I find the nearest Metro?" may not manage to travel very far, but should get a good read.

Metropolitan Line – Metropolitan should not be confused with its Italian equivalent Neapolitan which has three colours rather than one. The only line having the privilege of extending beyond Zone 6 once upon a time to Zone D, but now more sensibly numbered and primarily designed for 'City Types' living in the leafy areas of Chesham, Amersham and Pinner to get to their high powered City jobs, quickly and without changing train. As with the District Line, one end splits into many parts and ends in four different places. At least if you are travelling into London in the morning the trains all go the same way. If you work in Amersham and, for reasons known only to yourself, live in the City of London, firstly, please do not fall asleep in the morning and secondly, what are you thinking of? You could move to Amersham and avoid the Tube journey.

Northern Line – Strangely, this line runs both north and south. This line is an older line and leaves the passenger much more shaken up, if used for any distance. Not only does this line have four ends, it also splits in the middle, increasing the chances of the unsuspecting traveller getting lost. There are many names that might work well for this line. Visiting such auspicious locations as Wimbledon and Oval – it could be known as the English Sporting Line. In honour of Clapham and Wimbledon, it could be known as the Common Line. Most appropriately, given that it is the line that has spawned one of the greatest games known to man, it should be renamed the 'Mornington Crescent Line (subject to the rule of the Euston Interchange)'.

Notes – On an Underground Map there are notes after some of the station names. Unfortunately, these are not always self-explanatory and I for one do not know what message I am supposed to take away. Some examples that have occurred follow:

"Change at Chalfont & Latimer on most trains" against Chesham. It doesn't tell me which ones not to change on or what happens if I don't. Does it mean in both directions? If the alternative is that I will end up in Amersham, why is there no note against Amersham?

"No Piccadilly Line service Uxbridge – Rayners Lane in the early Mornings" against Rayners Lane. What do they count as early? Is it 1am to 3am or do the mean 7am to 8am – this would make a fundamental difference. Is there a service in the other direction?

"Also served by Piccadilly Line trains early mornings and late evenings" written against Turnham Green. In this instance, I am not sure why they are telling me, as that is the assumption I would have made from reading the map, which makes me think I must be reading the map incorrectly.

"Mondays to Saturdays open until 23.45 Sundays open until 23.15" written against Terminal 4 Heathrow. It doesn't however tell me from when – midnight for example would make you wonder why they close at all, whereas 7am might mean I can't get in when I needed to.

"Special fares apply for single and return tickets to and from this station" written against Harrow and Wealdstone. Now I am presuming they aren't offering special discounts to console the traveller, because that is the start point or end point of their journey. Why not create a separate zone for it and treat it in the same way as the old zone A to D stations?

"No entry from the street on Sundays 1300 – 1730 (exit and interchange only)" written against Camden Town, why? It's the same with Covent Garden. That says, "Exit only on Saturdays 1300 – 1700". What if I wanted to exit at another time? Am I forced to remain below ground until my appointed time slot? It is a great thing about England, the way we deal with being busy. What do we do? We close, so that the problem goes away. Quick the station's going to be busy, don't put on more staff, don't put on extra trains – close up instead – that'll solve the problem.

Off peak – the times you don't need to travel or, if you do need to travel, Tube trains don't run.

Oyster card – a method of bulk buying tickets rather than a card that can be exchanged for aphrodisiacs or the opportunity to discover precious stones.

Passengers – fellow psychopaths, or for those looking happy and unconcerned about being so closely pressed up against each other– lovers.

Passengers – The alternative definition is poor downtrodden travellers trying to make the best of a bad situation.

Peak – Any time you thought of travelling.

Piccadilly Line – Deceptive line with Piccadilly Circus almost exactly in the middle. The line stretches from Cockfosters in the north, through central London, before splitting (at Acton Town) for no apparent reason in two completely different directions and going to both Uxbridge and Heathrow – that is not one you want to get confused about. Trying to start your summer vacation to Florida in Uxbridge may not be all it's cracked up to be.

Platform – This is the area at the side of the track enabling passengers to wait for trains, while being tormented by large advertising hoardings showing glimpses of the real world away from the soulless confines of the Tube. Platforms are often on one side of the track, although putting a platform on the other side of the track with no exit would be tantamount to cruelty. Beware finding you are waiting for a train while standing on one of the disused platforms as you may have a long wait.

Pricing – The pricing leaflet that was in operation was a 'simple' guide for travellers running to sixteen pages, including options with footnotes referring to better options and was incomprehensible to many people, this was further confused by the Oyster Card with its maximum pricing guarantee. Now, however, you can get simple information using the web.

Queue – line of people, usually comprised of English nationals, forming often for no apparent reason other than the person at the front has stopped. Others then join, mistakenly believing they are waiting politely for some particular event or activity. In the meantime, most non-English have gone round the obstruction and bought their tickets, got on the train and completed their travel, wondering what all the English people were standing around waiting for.

Rats – furry creatures playing tag between the rails.

Rucksack – Useful device for carrying the many essential items required for Tube travel and compulsory for student travellers.

Seat – Place to allow commuters to travel comfortably, alternatively, mythical resting place rarer than hens' teeth during prime travelling time and adding to the congestion by taking up a greater floor area than intimate travelling passengers are likely to occupy. Theoretically to be given up for more needy passengers, although in this case to be effective the more needy passenger may need to be a 5' 10" leggy blond with a large bust and general good looks. It may also work if you are a very large menacing looking bloke and use fear to secure a seat.

Sleep – the longest journey without changes is from West Ruislip to Epping that should, if the average speed noted below holds true, take over an hour and a half. This is therefore the best journey to take if you want a relatively undisturbed sleep in the comfort of a Tube train. Unless, that is, you can find a Circle Line train scheduled to do multiple laps before being taken out of service.

Speed – the average speed including stopping at stations is 20.5mph. This may mean on those lines with few stations you travel quite slowly and for those with lots of stations you speed along in between in order to keep up. Alternatively, in the world of the Tube it may actually mean a different definition of average. Perhaps the trains most frequently run at this speed.

Standing room – This is the area on a train where a traveller can at least put both feet on the ground. As with seats, during rush hour, this may also be rarer than said hen's teeth and intimacy with fellow known and unknown passengers will be a prerequisite of travel.

Station – This is a point along a line (see above) that an Underground train stops at, to reshuffle its passengers. To confuse the issue some may be Ghost Stations or be merely a figment of yours and the cast of Eastenders' imaginations.
Subway – name used in many parts of the world to denote Tube or Underground. This is not to be confused with the fast food outlet of the same name.

Terminates – word used to describe the activity of a train at the end of the Line. Why not say, "This is the last stop"? It conjures up an image of the train disintegrating around you, leaving you unceremoniously dumped on the rails underneath.

Ticket – a necessary item to permit travel. Attempts to buy tickets on a Monday morning are discouraged, just in case the machines and ticket offices are busy. Suggesting you don't buy a ticket on a Monday morning is an effective way of reducing the 'longest queuing times' for tickets, but not from the commuters perspective.

Ticket Barrier – This is a machine into which you insert a valid ticket to enter the Underground system. When you reach your destination, you re-enter your ticket to escape. Sadly, if you needed a receipt, unless you bought a Travelcard that is valid for multiple journeys, the barrier will have eaten all evidence of your having used the Tube. Have a nice day.

Ticket Machines – These are confusing pieces of

apparatus allowing you to purchase your ticket without going to the Ticket Office (see below). It takes a significant amount of time to work out where to put your money, whether you want single or return, peak or off peak and in which zones you are travelling. Then you still have to find the station you are looking for on the list (St Pancras was and may still be under K for Kings Cross not S for St or P for Pancras). This is more than enough for a long irate queue to form behind you, baying for blood. (See also queue.)

Ticket Office – Locations at which you can be relieved of your money before being told that the train you wanted to travel on has been cancelled. Normally these are located below ground, which you would think for an underground would be an obvious choice. However, this is not something you should take for granted. To confuse the unsuspecting traveller, while doing the work at Kings Cross for the Channel Tunnel Rail Link for some unknown reason the ticket offices were moved above ground. This resulted in thousands of travellers walking down to the Underground before having to turn round and go back up the stairs to buy a ticket. The majority of the automatic ticket machines, also located above ground, being out of order, increased the confusion. The machines that were working gave instructions on unreadable screens.

Time (Tube) – an irrational warping of reality, caused by an absurd determination to stick to the timetable (see Timetable) (see also Late).

Timetable – a mythical sheet of times designed to cause

optimism in jaded travellers.

Trains – vehicles now powered by electricity and used to transport millions of people around London. There are around 500 in use at any one time and I have in my head the idea that it would be fun to create a complete model replica of the Tube and see if I can get them all running at once. I wonder what scale it would have to be to fit in the spare room? Of course, there wouldn't be much to see from the outside, as for the most part, they would all be running inside tunnels.

Tube - vehicle running on tracks underground (see Underground) through tube like tunnels, except where it runs 'over ground' and not in a tunnel.

Underground – name for the transport system running below London except where it travels above-ground. This is also known as The Tube. In some countries, this is more commonly known as The Metro or The Subway.

Victoria Line – Line passing through Victoria Station. Confusingly on this basis both the District and Circle Lines could also be called the Victoria Line. Interestingly links with proportionately more mainline rail lines than any other line and should on this basis perhaps be renamed the 'Mainline Escape Route Line'.

Waterloo and City Line – Ridiculously short line apparently with only two stops, Waterloo at one end and you would think City at the other, but you would be wrong. The other end is Bank – so why not call it Waterloo and Bank Line? It goes nowhere that cannot be reached by another route, but it does it faster and more directly – as long as you want to go to Bank or Waterloo and happen to be starting at the other point. This line is testament to the influence that powerful people with money can have, as compared to the likes of you and me. This is particularly evident with regard to me, as they took the section of line I needed to use out of service when they closed the end of the Jubilee line at Charing Cross.

West – As with East, this is a direction commonly seen on signs, particularly associated with one side of the road or the other. Rarely shown in conjunction with any clue to help you work out which one you wanted. This brings to mind the old question, "Why did the chicken cross the road?" In this case, the answer becomes "Because he followed the Underground signs and came out in the wrong place."

Zones – These are six areas covering London in concentric circles, adding to the confusion of Tube travel. Not to be confused with the four additional Zones tagged onto the north-west corner of the map that do not bother to become circles.

Conclusion

We have now travelled together around the vagaries of the Tube network. We have lingered over the perfume of the Tube. We have admired the dress sense of its passengers and we have been fascinated by the Underground's ability to transport so very many people within such bijou spaces. We have also appreciated the intimacy and the intricacy of its complex set up and revelled in the idiosyncrasies that we all hate to love. We have found in its culture, amusement and necessity and been grateful that when all is said and done it is a darn sight more enjoyable to use than modern day air travel, but maybe that's the subject for another book.

Given that within this book I have identified a number of games to play to pass the time while travelling, it seems appropriate to end with a classic culmination of a game that the Tube's confusion has spawned.

And so having called at Totteridge and Wealdstone, Temple, Lancaster Gate, Embankment via Piccadilly Circus, Greenford, Stonebridge Park and finally Bow Road, playing rule 42 and the Waterloo connection it is time to call out once again, 'Mornington Crescent'.

OTHER BOOKS BY THE AUTHOR

Novels
The Appearance of Truth
The Lifetracer
Alfie's Woods

Humour
Alfie's Diary
Lovers Take Up Less Space
Pet Dogs Democratic Party Manifesto

Non-fiction
Negotiation Skills for Lawyers
From Story Idea to Reader

Alfie Dog Fiction
Taking your imagination for a walk

visit our website at www.alfiedog.com

Join us on Facebook
http://www.facebook.com/AlfieDogLimited